STOP DOOMSCROLLING

HOW TO BREAK THE CYCLE TO RELIEVE STRESS, DECREASE ANXIETY, AND REGAIN YOUR LIFE

ROBERT WEST

ANNUS MIRABILIS
PUBLISHING

CONTENTS

Introduction   5

1. What is Doomscrolling?   11
2. Why We Doomscroll   18
3. How It Affects Your Mental Health   32
4. How It Affects Your Physical Health   42
5. How It Affects Your Social Life   54
6. How Did We Get Here and How to Tell if You're a   64
   Doomscroller
7. How to Stop Doomscrolling   75
8. Rewiring Your Mind   84
9. Retuning Your Body   94
10. Regaining Your Friends   119

Final Words   125

INTRODUCTION

You know the drill: the alarm goes off, and what's the first thing you reach for? Your telephone so you can check your social media feeds. And what do you see? How many are dead from the latest illness or disaster, the next storm being supercharged by the climate crisis, the latest meltdown in the financial sector, and so on and so on. It's just one bad piece of news after the next, but you're hooked. Worst of all, it leaves you with an impending sense of doom to carry you through your day.

Take it from me because I know firsthand what doomscrolling can do to your life. I suffered from the negative effects of my constant hunger for doom and gloom. I found myself almost constantly depressed, and I felt anxious about everything in my life and in the world around me. All I could think about was how the world is just going to hell in a handbasket. It made me feel helpless and hopeless.

It took a physical toll too. I stopped exercising and started eating more. I gained weight, and I kind of just stopped caring. I kept thinking, "What's the point?" There's a new disaster every day, there's social unrest because nothing much ever changes, and the pundits are always sounding the alarm about the financial sector. Everything just seems so bad, and there's not much I can do about it.

That's how I felt. I was deeply depressed, and my anxiety was through the roof. I was certain I would be homeless in the midst of a pandemic while a category 5 hurricane was striking. I don't even live near the coast! I just felt like nothing was going right nor would it ever. It was so bad, my friends stopped doing anything with me, and even my wife avoided me. I can't blame them. I wasn't very much fun to be around.

My conversations consisted of the latest catastrophe, or all the things we should all be afraid of in the coming days, months, and years. I remember how my friends would try to make a joke about it all, but I was having none of it. I couldn't fathom that they would be so cavalier when the sky was literally falling around us. It just didn't occur to me that the problem might be mine.

When I realized how bad things had gotten, I knew that I finally had to take action to break the spell. I couldn't go on living with the hopeless worldview I was creating. I had to make a change. It wasn't easy, but I am so much happier now that I've gotten free of my doomscrolling habit. If you're trapped in this kind of negative cycle, I want you to know you can change it. I did, and I want to help you do it too.

But what exactly is doomscrolling?

While we'll examine that question more fully in Chapter One, a brief definition is that doomscrolling, or doomsurfing as it's also called, refers to obsessively scrolling your social media feeds looking for the next sign of our doom. Though the exact origins of the term are unclear, most sources credit Canadian journalist Karen Ho with coining the term. She says, however, that she spotted it first on a Twitter post in October 2018. Whoever coined the term, the origins of why we do it have their roots in our distant, evolutionary past.

Being hungry for more information is something that's quite literally hard-wired into our biology. When our ancestors were roaming the savannah, being hyper-vigilant for the very real and very immediate threats was a necessity if they wanted to survive. If you found signs of danger, that was something worth knowing and remembering so you could avoid problems in the future.

Fast forward to our modern world where we get constant streams of information coming from all parts of the globe. There are very real threats, but there are also significant differences between our modern situation and that of our distant ancestors. First, when our ancestors located a threat, there was usually something they could do as individuals to confront or avoid the problem. The threats facing us in the modern world are often something that requires collective rather than individual action, and the dangers we're hearing about are frequently halfway around the globe from where we are located.

That's the second problem--though the information generates the same anxiety in us, it's often something that doesn't represent a direct threat to us. It's a threat to the people on the other side of the world, but not to us. Before the advent of modern technology, you wouldn't have known about a hurricane hitting the Philippines or an Ebola epidemic in Ghana. You would have only known about the threats in your immediate area, and these were something you might be able to respond to or avoid. But that's not the case anymore.

There have always been dangers to which the human species has had to respond, but before social media and 24/7 news cycles, you only heard about what was happening in your area. Now, it's a veritable onslaught of bad news from every corner of the world, and that kind of constant negativity takes a toll on your mental and physical health. It also can result in lost friendships and maybe even your marriage or romantic partnership.

After doing a lot of research into just what happens when you develop a habit for that negative newsfeed, I want to share what I've learned with you so that you can break the habit too. You'll be surprised at just what doomscrolling does to your mind and your body. Seeking out danger so you can survive is inborn in every organism, but the obsession we humans can develop because of our technology is over the top.

Mix our hard-wired hunger for constant information with worldwide pandemics, political upheaval, and social unrest, and you've got the makings of a deep depression. Our social feeds are full of conflicting 'facts' and rapidly changing landscapes, and that puts a huge demand on our cognitive processing as we try to make sense of it all. What's more, there's no overarching narrative to help us understand what's going on. It's all confusion and illusion, and that simply compounds the stress and anxiety we already feel as we strive to survive in our world.

You see, while the act of doomscrolling might make you feel informed, it doesn't actually help with anything. It doesn't stop the doom, and it really only makes you feel overwhelmed. The recent global crisis is a perfect case in point. No amount of doomsurfing social media and the internet could stop the pandemic, keep a single person from losing their job, or change the state of the economy. What it could do, however, is make you feel burned out, and it could even cause a decline in mental health at a time when we need people to keep their wits about them.

If any of this describes how you've felt as you obsessively scroll through your social media feeds, then this book can help you. Join me on a different quest for information as we explore doomscrolling and the impact it has on your health and well-being. We'll also discover just how to break that nasty habit so you can feel better both physically and mentally, and so you can truly discern just what actions you can take to address problems that are a part of your real life rather than your virtual life. As the ancient Chinese general Sun Tzu said, "Know thy enemy," so let's begin by understanding doomscrolling in all its forms.

1

WHAT IS DOOMSCROLLING?

Doomscrolling refers simply to your tendency to surf the net or scroll through news feeds and social media feeds looking for bad news. You feel positively drawn to continue doing it no matter how bad the news is or how irrelevant it is to your own life. It's something that's really taken on a life of its own with increasing isolation in our modern world. It's all too easy nowadays to work from home, and that can leave you isolated as you obsessively scroll through those news feeds.

You doomscroll about all kinds of things including pandemics, racial injustice, natural disasters, wars, and political unrest. Most, if not all of that, is something you can't do anything about on an individual level, or it's something you're already acting on personally, but the overall situation hasn't changed much. Much of it is something that's not even relevant to your situation. In other words, it doesn't represent an immediate threat, but you love it, and in fact, can't get enough of it.

One doomscroller notes he wakes each day hopeful for what is to come, but the first thing he does is reach for his telephone so he can throw himself into the abyss of negative news. And with that, there goes any hope he had for the day. It's a captivating thing to do. We're all drawn into that same void, and it's something that really has no historical precedent.

While our ancestors needed to know the dangers in their area, and indeed, we still need to know those that affect us, never has there been this combination of global access to information combined with individual isolation. The recent pandemic has left many people home alone with nothing more to do than scroll through their social media feeds and scan the internet for more information. What's more, our brains are hardwired to look for the negative. If it's bad news, you want to know all about it.

The problem with doomscrolling isn't the desire to stay informed or keep updated on the latest news, but when you do it in excess, just like anything else, it becomes an addiction. What's more, most people don't even realize that they're doing it. You have a question, you want an answer, and you assume getting that answer will make you feel better. So, you keep scrolling and scrolling until you just feel miserable. It can really change the way you look at the world around you.

Most people assume that if they understand the situation, they will gain a better sense of control over what to do, but doomscrolling doesn't actually give you control over anything. You usually just end up feeling more anxious, isolated, and depressed. While doom-scrolling existed prior to the pandemic, it has certainly picked up steam with so many people staying at home and having extra time on their hands for surfing the net.

How Many People are Doomscrolling?

The answer to that question is pretty much everyone, but new studies show that as the news regarding the 2020 pandemic increased so did American college students' phone use and their anxiety levels (Huckins et al., 2020). And it's not just an American habit. A survey of approximately 24,000 people in Russia showed that as people read more coronavirus-related news they became increasingly anxious, and this was above and beyond their normal anxiety levels (Nekliudov et al., 2020).

Another study that included thousands of German participants showed comparable results; the more they increased their news consumption, the more they experienced a sense of depression and increased anxiety (Bendau et al., 2020). Yet another study conducted prior to the pandemic showed the same results for Lebanese partici-pants. They experienced increased anxiety and insomnia when they obsessively read through their social media feeds (Malaeb et al., 2020). Thus, it's a cross-cultural phenomenon, or perhaps more aptly put, it's a human thing and it doesn't really matter what crisis is currently in the news. When you're doomscrolling, you'll find the bad news no matter what the topic.

Why Do We Keep Going When the News is So Bad?

Ah, that's a nifty little advertising trick. You see, every now and again as you're scrolling, you run across something positive. Maybe it's a cute meme or a motivational headline. Maybe it's just an attractive person, but it breaks the negative feed to give you a little taste of positive. It's that occasional reward, something psychologists refer to as a variable reinforcement schedule, which keeps you going down the doomscrolling path.

By rewarding you at unpredictable times, it prompts you to keep on seeking the next reward. It's the same principle used by casinos. You sporadically win when playing that slot machine, and that keeps you playing. Just like the slot machine, Twitter's got an infinite rolling scroll. What's more, we all--introverts and extroverts alike--crave connection to others. Those connections have been particularly limited during the Covid-19 pandemic, so when we read posts from our friends, regardless of the content, we seek that connection.

Your buddy may be rage-tweeting about some terrible injustice, something out of your control altogether, but it's the connection that keeps you scrolling. In that way, the 'social' in social media acts like fuel for the fire. We've all felt isolated to varying degrees during these challenging times, and we're simply seeking that connection. We also believe that by learning more, we'll get clarity on the situation. Unfortunately, the clarity never comes.

Instead of clarity and control, we're left feeling ever more helpless, unproductive, anxious, angry, and depressed. What's more, we even end up feeling less connected not only with our loved ones, but with ourselves as well. It's really an all-around tough situation.

Why is it in the News Now?

You might never have heard about doomscrolling until recently. That's because it has really begun to cause problems on a mass scale since the onset of the pandemic. In fact, as of the time of this writing, Twitter's usage has increased by 24 percent since the pandemic started and Facebook's usage is up by some 27 percent. Some users, like K (the name is withheld to protect the individual's privacy), check their feeds between 10 and 15 times daily.

The pandemic has exacerbated doomscrolling habits for a few reasons. First, there's certainly no shortage of bad news in 2020. The pandemic hits, people are dying, the economy tanks, people are losing their jobs, and many are standing in food lines just to give their families enough to eat. That sure sounds like doomsday to me!

Another reason doomscrolling habits are increasing, however, is that many news outlets, such as the New York Times, are offering their pandemic coverage for free. While that helps truly keep you informed, it also increases the abundance of negative headlines available for consuming.

K links her doomscrolling habit to a need for reassurance. She doesn't want to get back into any area of her life until there is a reliable treatment or vaccine to protect her. So, she obsessively checks her news feeds looking for something positive to report. But the problem is our brains simply aren't wired to look for good news. They're wired to find any kind of threat, and that's what draws your eye to the negative headlines, of which, as we've noted, there are plenty.

K reports that while she tells herself she is looking for good news to reduce her anxiety, the result is that she feels worse after doomscrolling. That hypervigilance just doesn't pay off in this scenario. Still, it is worth noting that some people find their doomscrolling habit to be a welcome distraction from their everyday life.

Take B, a 49-year-old man who lives in Louisiana. He doomscrolls to escape from the drudgery of his work life. He finds that knowing bigger problems exist on the national or global scale helps keep him from thinking so much about the possibility of losing his own job. For him, his habit helps him feel better.

C also finds that scrolling has improved his life. He has met many people through his scrolling habit, and he credits them with changing his worldview. He feels he has become a better person who is able to engage in a healthier way. So, it's not all doom and gloom, but by far, the overwhelming majority of people who doomscroll report negative consequences as opposed to positive results in their lives.

Look, it's normal to want answers, particularly in these uncertain times, but as we doomscroll in the isolation forced upon us by the pandemic, we are unable to tap into the collective sense-making that we usually rely on for answers. Moreover, conspiracy theories are flourishing, and while we flick through those social media feeds over and overlooking for the latest headlines, we are constantly being flooded with more bad news than good news--if it bleeds, it leads, right?

Most of the time, any rapidly unfolding news story means bad news. And while it is important to stay informed, the obsessive hunt for information combined with the human tendency to pay more attention to bad news can warp our worldview. It can leave us feeling hopeless as well as helpless, and it makes it easier for us to overlook the good news that's out there too, or to reasonably assess that to which we're being exposed. But why do it? That's what we'll talk about in more detail in the next chapter.

2

WHY WE DOOMSCROLL

Humans have been evolutionarily hardwired to do all kinds of things that really no longer serve us in the modern world. When our comparatively frail ancestors were struggling to survive in a wilderness full of large carnivores and fast herbivores, every bit of information they could learn about threats to their survival was imperative to staying alive.

Let's face it, as compared to our predators and our prey, we're pretty weak. We can't run faster than either, and we don't have claws or sharp fangs to fight back with when attacked or to kill with when hunting. But the one thing we do have going for us is our brain. It's quite simply gigantic when compared to our body size. Sure, an elephant has an overall larger brain, but when you compare it to the elephant's body size, it's really not that big.

In our case, we have a smaller body size, but a brain that is approximately 2 percent of our body weight. That's compared to an elephant's brain, which is about 0.1 percent of its body weight. Our brain consumes, however, approximately 20 percent of the nutritional resources we ingest. That tells you how complex and vital it is for our survival. For our body to dedicate that much of our nutritional resources to one organ illustrates its importance.

Our brain is so complex because it is our only real advantage in a dangerous world. But how exactly did it get that way? It's actually a fascinating story. You see, Charles Darwin--the guy who came up with the idea of survival of the fittest--posited that should an animal have genes that are not compatible with the environment in which it lives, it will fail to pass on its genes and eventually fall by the wayside as a casualty of the 'war of nature.' So, to pass on your genes, you have to survive, and to survive, you have to be able to both avoid predators and catch or find whatever it is that you eat.

In the case of humans, that meant optimizing our intelligence. For our purposes here--that of doomscrolling--the important neurobiological evolutionary mechanisms we're talking about are those that would have helped our ancestors avoid predatory threats. Now, eons of avoiding predators like lions have equipped us well for survival, and they've made us highly adaptable to changing environmental threats.

Fight or Flight

You might have heard of the fight or flight response of the human nervous system. This is the part of your brain that prepares you to either put up your dukes or beat a hasty retreat in the event of a threat. Recent research has shown that this primitive brain system is integrated and interconnected with the forebrain structures, like the prefrontal cortex, that are involved with our complex cognitive functions, our so-called 'higher thinking' centers. That's important because human survival intelligence likely also involves some unique adaptations, such as being cunning, understanding the sinister desires of others, and strategizing in complex social environments. Those are all higher thinking cognitive functions that would need to be embedded in our primitive brain's responses to perceived threats.

Human Threat Assessment

Some animals, and humans are among them, are able to navigate multiple habitats. But those that do must have an adaptable set of cognitive and behavioral systems that allow them to rapidly recognize different types of threats in novel environments, both externally and internally.

Humans are veritable masters at adapting to changing environments and novel circumstances. Moreover, our brains have flexible systems that allow us to make sophisticated predictions regarding variable situations and to employ learning strategies to avoid danger. In other words, we have an enhanced ability to quickly learn what is important in a given environment and to optimize our behaviors in order to fulfill new goals associated with survival needs,

So, for example, in a culturally modified environment where money has become a requirement for obtaining resources associated with survival, we have been able to recognize that and modify our behaviors accordingly to meet the goal of obtaining money to fulfill our survival needs. That's actually pretty astounding. Imagine trying to teach your dog that he has to make money in order to eat.

Because we have culturally modified our environments, there is now a big difference between what our species originally evolved to handle and our modern environment. And the extensive neurobiological flexibility we've developed in response to the many unique environments we've encountered is precisely what renders us vulnerable to problems like depression and anxiety. Simply put, our ability to recognize potential future threats is great if we're talking about lions and tigers and bears, but not so good for our mental health in our modern world. It can lead to obsession and constant anxiety.

Human Survival Optimization System

You can probably start to see how this all relates to doomscrolling, but if not, bear with me, you will. What we're talking about here relates to the long-term survival of any species. To endure, you must be able to learn from and respond to real, immediate threats, and potential future threats as well. That involves using the following strategies (Mobbs et al., 2015):

- Prediction
- Prevention
- Threat-orientation
- Threat assessment
- Rapid reaction

The systems that regulate these strategies include your ability to cognitively appraise the situation, your ability to sense the internal state of your body and make adjustments, and your metabolic drives which fuel the rapid reaction. These are integrated with your learning systems that help you make judgments regarding the probability of a particular threat as well as to vicariously learn through watching the problems that befall your peers (Mobbs et al., 2015). To better understand how these systems work and where doomscrolling comes into play, let's look at these five strategies more closely.

Prediction Strategies

This is catastrophizing: assuming the worst. It's where you consciously predict and run simulations of a potential threat. Typically, it occurs from a safety context, and it helps you prepare yourself for a potential danger or crisis. You can then modify your behavior, plan an escape, and take steps to avoid the possible danger. These strategies result in more precautionary behaviors like increased alertness, environmental surveillance, and attempting to avoid the threat before it is actually encountered.

You can see all of these strategies in play with the 2020 COVID-19 crisis. You perceive the potential threat of a future infection--you run simulations including being put on a ventilator--and you take steps to modify your behavior, plan an escape from threat, and avoid the possible danger. These steps include wearing a mask and social distancing (modifying your behavior), and self-isolating (planning an escape from the threat and avoiding the danger).

Our ancestors' prediction strategies included seeking the safety of group living, something the current crisis prompts us to avoid. You can see a conflict there that can create stress. We're evolutionarily geared toward seeking out our group, but this is one instance where the group is the problem.

It's worthwhile to consider what this teaches us about our brain. The complex predictions we commonly invoke require imagination, simulation, and analogical reasoning. We constantly engage in 'what if' scenarios. What if I get the virus? What if I lose my job? What if I can't pay the bills? And, in response to those simulations, we attempt to devise multiple strategies for dealing with each; that is, we develop Plan A, Plan B, Plan C, and so on.

Prevention Strategies

These are the strategies we employ to try to prevent ourselves from falling prey to a perceived threat. Historically, living in groups creates the perception that we are safer since it reduces our odds of being singled out by a predator, but when the predator is a virus, group living can actually be detrimental to our survival. That's perhaps one reason why we're experiencing the high level of anxiety in the current crisis.

Everything, right down to our very cells, is prompting us to seek out the safety of the group, and yet, we cognitively know that is precisely what we should not do with the specific threat of a pandemic. The angst that creates helps to drive our obsessive behaviors, including doomscrolling. But group living is not our only prevention strategy.

The second prevention strategy humans have employed throughout evolutionary history is that of niche construction. This refers to our ability to alter our environment. In the case of a predatory attack, if you can predict it, you can prepare for it to increase your likelihood of survival. Given the current viral threat, that includes things like wiping down your groceries to kill any viral particles present, cleaning your home with detergents known to kill the virus, and so on.

Our brain is excellent at envisioning and producing advanced strategies for minimizing the threat. But imagine a brain stretched to the breaking point with multiple threats it perceives from doomscrolling. Your poor brain is trying to develop preventative strategies to everything from cataclysmic floods to political coups. It's exhausting just to think about it.

Threat Orienting Strategies

One of the main threats orienting strategies employed by many organisms is that of directing your attention to the threat. But this can lead to the cessation of ongoing behaviors and a sort of freezing, like a deer in the headlights, as you orient your attention to the threat in question. Moreover, the other side of directing your attention to the threat is that of remaining vigilant to the possibility of a threat. This requires heightened vigilance, which is very costly from an energy perspective.

Under normal circumstances, it would only be employed when you predict a high-risk threat; however, in our modern world, there are many high-risk threats that can capture our attention. The fact that they may be happening half a world away isn't something our brain processes as part of this system. That's one of the main problems with doomscrolling; it commands your attention and leads to hyper-vigilance which produces not only that deer in the headlights feeling as you scroll through your feeds, but it also causes you to disengage from your normal goal-seeking behaviors. The problem is, though, that this system is stimulated into action as you doomscroll regardless of how real or immediate the threat may actually be to you personally.

The threat orientation system also works to prepare you biologically for a response--the fight or flight response--and to help reduce the possibility of a surprise attack given your enhanced vigilance. In this way, it's clear that the system involves more than just where you put your attention. It includes your perceptions and memory as well as your attention. Of course, there is room for error in this system. There are two kinds of errors.

The first error possibility is that you fail to react when a threat is imminent--this is the worst scenario since you could pay with your life for that mistake. The other type of error is a false alarm. From an evolutionary perspective, it's better to have a false alarm than it is to have no alarm when a threat is actually present. But, as you might imagine, in our doomscrolling modern world, increased anxiety generates a higher incidence of those false alarms, and the frequent triggering of the system generates more anxiety. It's a negative feedback loop that has you constantly nervous and exhausted.

Threat Assessment Strategies

Once a threat is detected, your brain now switches to evaluation mode. This is where it considers the context in which the threat is encountered and appraises the danger level. Additionally, it begins to strategize response options. To your mind, this happens almost instantaneously, but there are actually several steps involved, some of which are happening at the same time as one another.

- *Post-encounter freezing*: When you first encounter a threat, the initial response is to freeze until you can properly assess the danger and determine the best response. Usually, it's best to wait until you fully understand the nature of the threat before responding.

- *Threat monitoring*: Once you've identified a threat and determined an appropriate response, you need to continue to monitor that threat to ensure the response has been effective. For example, you see a dangerous animal in the vicinity, let's say a poisonous snake, and you determine the best course of action is to let it go on its way. But, of course, you need to continue to monitor the animal to ensure it is leaving your vicinity. This results in a heightened level of alertness. In our modern world, as we're exposed to a constant stream of negative news, that turns into anxiety even though you consciously know the threat is not relevant to your situation.

- *Safety seeking*: This strategy involves just what it sounds like, you seek safety from the threat, but it also involves monitoring the location to ensure it remains safe. You actually see this strategy engaged in people with anxiety disorders. They frequently will check exits in buildings or look for the proximity of a hospital as part of seeking a safe refuge from the threats they perceive. Knowing you've got a safe location to take refuge reduces fear, but when you're exposed to virtual threats, it can be difficult to establish a safe refuge.

- *Threat value*: This refers to the threat value you give the situation. You may decide it is a high level of threat or a low level, but the regions of the brain that are active as you make this determination are the same regions tied to anxiety, memory, and response formation. While you can more accurately determine the threat value when we're talking about a lion in the bushes, it gets significantly more difficult when you're reading about a hurricane hitting the Philippines. You might not be in the danger zone, but your anxiety might be heightened as you see the devastation and hear the news regarding how climate change is affecting these storms. The latter can represent a threat to you as well. As you can see, it gets complicated. What's more, the inability to accurately assess the threat value can, in and of itself, cause anxiety.

- *Predicting the actions of the threat*: This is where your brain produces multiple simulations to attempt to predict the actions of the threat. As you can imagine, this plays a huge role in how you respond to any given threat. It includes multiple areas of the brain working together to assess incoming sensory information for predicting threat movements. It gets much more complicated when you're attempting to predict the possible actions of threats for which you have limited incoming sensory information. So, when you're doomscrolling, your brain prompts you to continue seeking more information for this system to be able to do its job. That's part of what keeps you seeking more news. You need the information to make adequate predictions, and without it, your anxiety increases.

- *Action preparation*: This also is self-explanatory, but the important thing to understand is all the brain has gone through to arrive at this point. Additionally, now the brain is creating a cascade of physical responses to get the body ready for action. As it relates to doomscrolling, your brain generates the physical responses repeatedly as you're being exposed to perceived threats you're reading about in your social media feeds. The process of repeatedly stimulating the fight or flight (sympathetic) nervous system is physically exhausting, which compounds the effects of the anxiety and depression you may also be experiencing.

Rapid Reaction

This is the final stage of responding to a threat. It's where you take steps to escape, avoid, or fight the threat. It can involve defensive actions, offensive actions, fleeing the threat, or actively or passively coping with the situation when no other action is possible. And this is another source of frustration in the case of doomscrolling.

Because of the nature of the 'threats' you encounter while obsessively scrolling for bad news, there's often no action you can take to alleviate your growing anxiety. That results in your brain prompting you to get more information, more clarity regarding the situation. But your brain won't find that satisfaction it's seeking. Instead, it finds more threats that ultimately leave it with less clarity, which serves to continue the cycle of seeking behavior. What's more, the constant seeking and exposure to threats that don't represent direct or immediate threats to you has a significant effect on the modulatory and learning systems that are also involved in this process.

Modulatory Systems

These are the systems in the brain that govern how you appraise and manage threat responses. When it's working efficiently, it tailors the responses to the specific circumstances of the threat. The idea here is that it gives you the highest likelihood of survival. The problem with doomscrolling is that your modulatory systems have difficulty appraising the threat, and therefore, you can't manage the response. This further has an effect on the intensity of your alertness and vigilance for threats. It also takes time from other activities. Because of the difficulty appraising the threat, your brain keeps prompting you to seek more information, resulting in obsessive behaviors.

Learning Systems

Normally, your brain learns from each threat, and it updates and modifies responses based on that learning. To learn, it's getting feedback from all of the systems involved in threat prediction, assessment, and response formation. With doomscrolling, however, these systems are undermined because of the nature of the perceived threats. That further impacts your brain's desire for more information. It's simply not getting the satisfaction it normally gets from a more traditional kind of threat.

If you were escaping a lion on the savannah, these systems would work together well to help you learn the most beneficial responses and the contexts in which the threats occur. But none of that is happening when you're doomscrolling. You're perceiving threats, but your brain is unable to adequately assess and respond because they are outside of your immediate environment. Our ancestors simply didn't know of any threats like that. They were only able to respond to what was happening in their immediate environment.

The inability to fully understand and assess your doomscrolling threats causes your brain to prompt you to seek more information, which keeps you scrolling through those feeds. As this happens repetitively, your brain forms a new habit. The formation of habits is something that results in a kind of automatic response in the brain.

Habit Formation

Habit formation involves three factors: the cue that triggers the habitual behavior, the behavior itself--called the habit routine--and the reward the brain gets for engaging in the habit routine. The reward usually involves a shot of the brain's feel-good chemical, dopamine.

In the case of doomscrolling, the cue that triggers the habit routine could be your alarm sounding in the morning. That's what causes you to begin scrolling your social media feeds. As you engage in the scrolling, you alternate between feeling more informed and needing more clarity or more information. You also get those periodic feel-good rewards like the cute meme or the image of an attractive person. All of this information seeking produces the dopamine reward response in your brain.

In the brain, there are specialized neurons associated with habits. They are activated with the cue, and they both then prompt you to engage in the habit routine as they simultaneously prevent any other habit routine from running at the same time. This helps you engage in the routine in a focused manner, without needing to really think about what you're doing.

When we're talking about habits like brushing your teeth in the morning, that's a good thing because it frees your brain to think about other things while you're engaged in the habit routine. But, when we're talking about a bad habit, like doomscrolling, the automatic nature of the habit serves to reinforce the bad behavior and make it more difficult for you to stop. That's why it can feel nearly impossible to stop doomscrolling. It's not, as we'll see, but changing that bad habit means staying focused and committed.

As you can imagine, all of this searching for bad news can take a serious toll on your mental and physical health. In fact, you might be surprised at just how much it can change the way you think about your life and the world around you. We'll look at the effects of doomscrolling on your mental health in the next chapter.

3

HOW IT AFFECTS YOUR MENTAL HEALTH

In the previous chapter, we discussed what is happening in your brain and how that stimulates you to continue the bad doom-scrolling habit, but those physical neurobiological responses and the information you're exposing yourself to can also affect your mood. This can have serious consequences for your mental health.

The nature of social media is such that the scroll never ends, and that prompts you to keep going. The current isolation due to the pandemic has caused Americans to spend as much as 50 percent more time surfing the net than they were previously. And that's in place of actually spending time with friends and family, something forbidden with the current crisis.

That means you're not only being exposed to a constant feed of negative news, you're also not getting together with friends and family members who might temper both your habit and your interpretation of what you're reading. You can easily spiral into an abyss of negative news that leaves you feeling ever more stressed, anxious, and depressed.

My habit started as a genuine interest in what was going on around the world. I told myself I was being a responsible citizen by staying informed. I guess that was my way of justifying my obsession. It wasn't long before I noticed the effect of my habit on my mood, but by then it felt like I couldn't stop. I found that I almost preferred doing that over anything else, including spending valuable time with my loved ones. That's not an uncommon feeling among doom-scrollers.

As you experience more anxiety, stress, and depression, that can lead to more hostility or heightened aggressive behaviors. Everything you're seeing online makes you just feel more helpless and hopeless. It gives you a sense that nothing can be done, and that makes you feel extremely frustrated and even agitated.

Though you may initially feel a sense of security derived from what you perceive of as being informed, that secure feeling is fleeting. You soon find that those feelings of frustration and agitation are leaving you feeling more isolated than the coronavirus has managed to do. You also will likely be more emotionally reactive as a result of the increasing sense of stress that you feel from all the negative information you're reading.

Eventually, you're left with a profound sense of doom and gloom which can even lead to clinical depression. All of this adds to the sense that you're completely helpless against the situation and that can stimulate another frenzy of information seeking. It's a vicious cycle that heightens your sense of frustration, agitation, loneliness, and despair.

Meanwhile, as we've seen, your brain is desperately trying to make sense of what is happening. It's prompting you for more information, but nothing you provide gives it the satisfaction it needs to shut the cycle down. You can't experience that sense of security you want nor can you even fully grasp the nature of the threat you think you're perceiving. You can't get clarity, you can't fully assess any threats you read about, and you feel completely out of control. It's a recipe for disaster, to say the least.

Learned Helplessness

Learned helplessness happens when a person is repeatedly confronted with uncontrollable, stressful situations, and even if it becomes possible for them to exercise a modicum of control in the situation, they don't do it. They end up learning that they are helpless, and they effectively give up trying to change things even if it is possible to do so.

This is essentially what is happening as you doomscroll. You are repeatedly being confronted with situations that are wholly out of your control to the extent that even if some action is possible, you don't take it. You have learned that you're helpless to what is happening. You can't change the path of that hurricane or get rid of racism in America or keep politicians from doing what you're opposed to. The sense of helplessness this generates gets to the point that even though you can vote against a politician or take individual action against racism, you may not do it, because in your mind, it won't make a difference. You're helpless.

As this goes on, it begins to affect your ability to make decisions in any part of your life. It can cause you to become passive when facing traumatic experiences, it can prevent you from learning more appropriate coping mechanisms, and of course, it causes your stress levels to soar. All of this increases your risk of depression and other mental health disorders.

Learned helplessness manifests itself as a person who doesn't use or even learn adaptive responses to challenging situations. This kind of person simply accepts that bad things are going to happen, and they won't be able to control them. Even if there is a possible solution, they are unable to appropriately resolve the problem.

There are many different ways you can learn helplessness, but with regard to doomscrolling, you are repetitively confronted with often devastating news over which you have absolutely no control. Even if you initially try to take actions to help--you start recycling, you reduce your carbon footprint, you organize an aid package to send to those hurricane victims, or you campaign for the candidate of your choice--you quickly realize that your actions are just a drop in an ocean of bad news. You decide there's no way it will help the situation, and so, you just give up. You have learned to be helpless, and that can have devastating effects on every area of your life.

Anxiety and Stress

In addition to learned helpless, and often along with it, doomscrolling heightens your level of anxiety and stress. It's not an exaggeration to say that there's a lot of bad news everywhere you look these days. It's all around all of us, and of course, the various media eat it up, which means so do you, but several researchers have documented the effects of this constant exposure to negative news.

One study examined the effects of such exposure following the 9/11 attacks. As that was unfolding, millions of people were watching it, and they continued watching repeated coverage of the attacks. Many were also subsequently exposed to graphic images associated with the Iraq War. A study in 2013 (Silver et al.) included 2,189 US citizens who were exposed to this media coverage between one and three weeks following 9/11. A smaller sample of those same people (1,322) were also studied upon the initiation of the Iraq War. The study was designed to measure participants' acute stress responses following negative media exposure.

The participants were followed for three years, and each year, their posttraumatic stress symptoms as well as any physical ailments were assessed. The study found that those individuals who were exposed to four or more hours each day of 9/11 media coverage in the early weeks following the attacks were more likely to develop health ailments in the next two to three years. Both exposure to the 9/11 and Iraq War media coverage was predictive for increased posttraumatic stress symptoms within two to three years following that exposure.

When the coronavirus pandemic began in 2020, these same researchers published an article that predicted there would be serious mental and physical health problems following the exposure to the negative news media about the virus. As it turned out, it was worse than they predicted. By the time of COVID-19, endless scrolling through social media feeds had become commonplace. Additionally, the pandemic was a slow-moving disaster, which meant people would be scrolling about the very real danger for a much longer time than what had happened with 9/11.

The fact that the danger is real and a possible threat, causes your brain to go into hypervigilance mode as you scan for more information to make yourself feel better. Imagine that you have a phobia about spiders--it's a common one--but now imagine that you're actually seeing spiders everywhere you look! Your brain is on the lookout for danger, and now you're seeing danger everywhere. As you can imagine, your anxiety goes through the roof. What's more, the information you find about the dangers in our modern world doesn't actually make you feel better about anything.

In fact, it becomes a vicious cycle. The more you learn about terrible things in the news, the more you worry about those bad things, and the more you then search for more news about those bad things. You're worried because you're seeing bad things in the news media which, in turn, are causing you to worry. The more anxious you are, the more likely you are to search for more news, and the more likely you are to become anxious when you actually find bad news. It becomes almost impossible to break free from this cycle.

The more you seek out information, the worse you feel about it, and because you feel worse, you seek out more information. This cycle of distress has been confirmed by research conducted following the 2013 Boston Marathon bombing as well as the 2016 Orlando Pulse night-club shooting (Thompson et al., 2019). The 2020 pandemic was worse because not only were people traumatized by the events that were unfolding, but they were also isolated at home where they frequently had little else to do but scroll through their news media feeds looking for information.

Effects of Prolonged Anxiety and Stress

It's clear that constant exposure to negative news causes increased stress and anxiety, but what does that do, particularly if it's over a prolonged period of time? Research has shown that there is an extensive overlap of the brain's circuitry involved with chronic anxiety, fear, and stress. Mah et al. (2016) found that when these emotions are experienced over the long-term, they can result in a variety of neuropsychiatric disorders including depression and even Alzheimer's disease.

When you're experiencing anxiety, your brain is flooding your body with stress hormones like cortisol. That has real physical effects including weakening your immune system and causing both metabolic and cardiovascular problems. But it can also lead to the atrophy (shrinkage) of the hippocampus in the brain. This area of the brain is vital for your long-term memory and your spatial navigation, that is, knowing where you're physically located relative to other people and things. It also negatively affects the prefrontal cortex. These effects account for the increased risk of neuropsychiatric problems.

There is a mixed response in the brain when the part of the brain active with emotional responses (amygdala) becomes overactive, and areas of the brain that help regulate those emotional responses by cognitively appraising the situation (the hippocampus and the prefrontal cortex) are suppressed. Thus, you become more emotionally reactive and the parts of your brain that would normally moderate those responses are less able to help do that. You can see where this is going. You become almost incapable of controlling your emotions which are running wild as your fear whips them into a frenzy. These changes can manifest in the form of the following symptoms:

- Worrying all the time
- An inability to control your worry
- Difficulty concentrating and paying attention
- Experiencing worries that are out of proportion with the problem
- An inability to relax
- Avoiding people or places
- Withdrawing from friends and family
- Feeling annoyed, irritated, or restless
- Difficulty sleeping

These are not completely irreversible changes, however, as there is evidence that the stress-induced damage to these parts of your brain can be treated with cognitive behavioral therapy and exercise. But some of the damage done is associated with accelerating the onset of Alzheimer's disease in people who have already been diagnosed with a mild cognitive impairment.

In fact, another study found that the effects of exposure to negative news can be mitigated by a progressive relaxation exercise. Szabo and Hopkinson (2007) found that subjects who were exposed to a 15-minute random newscast exhibited increased anxiety and a total mood disturbance as well as a change from a positive affect (expression) to a negative effect. One group of these subjects was then led through a 15-minute progressive relaxation exercise whereas the other group was given a 15-minute lecture. The group that experienced the progressive relaxation exercise returned to the pre-newscast levels of anxiety and mood, but the group that was given a lecture remained unchanged.

This shows two things: first, exposure to the news triggers negative psychological feelings, and second, those feelings can be buffered, but only by directed psychological interventions like progressive relaxation exercises. In other words, a distraction designed to divert the participants' attention didn't lower their anxiety levels. It was only the progressive relaxation exercise that was successful in doing that. Thus, help is available, but it must take a certain form.

Catastrophizing

There's more to the way that doomscrolling damages your psychological wellbeing than just the anxiety it causes. Johnston and Davey (1997) found that participants exposed to negative news feeds not only showed increases in anxiety and sad mood, but they also demonstrated a significant increase in the tendency to catastrophize about something they were worried about personally. In other words, exposure to the negative news happening around us causes us to project that negativity onto our own personal concerns, including those not relevant to the content of the news feed. And all of this was evident after viewing just a 14-minute news bulletin. Imagine what happens after days, weeks, months, or even years of daily doomscrolling.

What's more, our depressed mood actually then triggers an information processing bias that favors threatening or negative information. And, when you're in a depressed mood state, it causes your brain to then call up memories that match your sad mood. That compounds your bad mood and triggers you to then seek out more depressing information. Talk about a hot mess!

Let's recap. Exposure to even a minimal amount of negative or neutral news dramatically changes your mood by specifically increasing anxiety and sad or bad moods. That anxiety and sadness can cause you to seek out more bad news to the point where you experience learned helplessness in the face of a dangerous world over which you have no control. This can literally damage your brain and increase your risk for more serious neuropsychiatric disorders like Alzheimer's disease.

It damages your working memory and decreases your brain's ability to cognitively appraise the situation. Moreover, the part of your brain that's associated with emotions becomes overactive and the parts of your brain that help to regulate emotions become underactive. In short, it leaves you emotional and unable to logically assess the threat. To make matters worse, your brain then starts to dredge up old memories of negative events that match your sad, emotional mood and you begin to catastrophize about your own personal problems. What more, as you do this repeatedly, it becomes a habit that feels almost impossible to break. Is it any wonder this starts to affect your personal relationships? These are just the mental effects of doomscrolling, but what it's doing to your physical health?

4

HOW IT AFFECTS YOUR PHYSICAL HEALTH

A s we've already seen, doomscrolling can cause a veritable cascade of effects on your mental health, and the same is true for your physical health. There are a number of direct and indirect effects on your physical health. Let's start with the initial stress response to bad news.

Sympathetic Nervous System Activation

The sympathetic nervous system is responsible for your body's response to a threat. It prepares you to either fight or flee a possible danger. As part of this response, your heart rate increases so that you are better prepared to run or become active in a confrontation. For the same reason, your breathing becomes more rapid so your body can feed your muscles with an increased demand for oxygen. Your blood pressure rises as your heart is pumping your blood more rapidly through your arteries and veins. Your muscles tense up in preparation for action and your eyes dilate so you can see better what is around you. All of this is automatic; you don't control it. In fact, you're usually not even aware it's happening.

Once the danger has passed, the parasympathetic nervous system kicks in and reverses those changes. Your breathing and heart rates decrease, your blood pressure is lowered, your muscles relax, and your eyes return to normal dilation. You also typically feel exhausted. The entire cycle of the physical response to a threat involves a lot of changes in your body over a very short period of time. If these systems are repeatedly activated, it can actually cause you to collapse. In fact, many modern-day hunters and gatherers use the repeated activation of the sympathetic nervous system to hunt animals by running them to death.

It's a technique called persistence hunting. It involves just jogging close enough to the animals to stimulate their sympathetic nervous system which causes them to run. They get away, but the hunter just keeps coming. After repeated activation of the flight response, an animal just collapses, and the hunter just needs to walk up to it and finish it off. That explains why you often feel exhausted after doomscrolling. What's more, it can cause you to delay going to bed at night and interfere with your sleep patterns. That only serves to increase your physical exhaustion.

Indirect Effects of Chronic Stress

When the sympathetic nervous system is activated, there are a number of hormonal changes that happen in the body. Your brain triggers the release of adrenaline, cortisol, norepinephrine, and several other hormones. All of these are helpful if you need to run away from that lion, but not so much if they're just being stimulated by your habit of obsessively scrolling your social media feeds for bad news. Moreover, when these hormones are released into your system on a repeated basis, they can cause serious health problems. Let's take a look at how this can negatively impact the various systems in the body.

Endocrine System

As we've mentioned, when you perceive a threat, your sympathetic nervous system kicks in to stimulate the release of hormones that help you either fight or flee from the threat. The system in your body that's associated with hormone production is called the endocrine system, and the part of the endocrine system that produces the endocrine stress response is the hypothalamic-pituitary-adrenal axis. Say what? Let's just say the HPA axis, that's much easier. This is the part of the endocrine system that actually stimulates the increased production of steroid hormones which are known as glucocorticoids. These include such hormones as cortisol.

The HPA axis response begins in the hypothalamus. This is the part of the brain that connects to the endocrine system. The hypothalamus signals a gland in your brain called the pituitary gland to produce stress hormones. The pituitary gland, also known as the master gland, then signals the adrenal glands--which are located above the kidneys-- to increase their production of cortisol. Cortisol then stimulates the release of glucose and fatty acids from the liver so that you will have enough fuel for your body to do what you need to do to escape the threat. It's also a potent anti-inflammatory hormone that reduces inflammation, so you won't be slowed down by pain. It is also possible that cortisol helps to consolidate fear-based memories so that you can avoid danger in the future.

Too much of a good thing, however, is not always a good thing. When your body produces too much cortisol in response to repeated exposure to threats and elevated levels of anxiety, such as results from doomscrolling, the effects of the hormone become maladaptive--that means bad. First, long-term cortisol production can result in almost the opposite of its beneficial short-term effects. It can cause you to become more sensitized to pain, and it can cause widespread inflammation and associated pain. Chronic inflammation has been associated with a number of physical problems including gastrointestinal upset, high blood pressure, and heart problems. Secondly, chronic production of cortisol might also be what is active in helping you recall those painful memories from your past which then serve to deepen your sadness and increase your anxiety (Hannibal and Bishop, 2014).

Musculoskeletal System

Of course, one of the first things you feel when you're stressed is your muscles tensing up. It's how your body guards against injury and pain. When you're suddenly stressed, your muscles tense up and then they release that tension once the situation has passed. But, with chronic stress, your muscles are tensed in a constant state of being guarded. When that happens, it can trigger other problems in your body.

One problem you might experience with chronic stress and muscle tension is a headache. It might even be a migraine headache, particularly if you tend to carry your stress in your shoulders and neck. Additionally, chronic muscle tension can produce pain in your lower back and your upper extremities. This can lead to musculoskeletal disorders that often result in chronic pain. What's more, it's not uncommon for people who feel pain to avoid physical activity that they fear will only serve to exacerbate the problem. That can cause the muscles involved to atrophy--shrink--and this disuse of the body can lead to other types of problems. Those individuals who maintain some level of moderate, supervised activity tend to recover better than people who avoid activity, but this can be a problem when you're continuing to engage in the activity that created the muscle tension in the first place.

Respiratory System

Your respiratory system is clearly vital for your health. It's how you take in oxygen and transfer it to your blood where it is then distributed to the cells in your body. In exchange for the oxygen, the respiratory system removes carbon dioxide waste. Quite simply, you breathe air in through your nose where it then passes through the larynx, down your trachea, and into your lungs. From there, the oxygen passes into your blood and the carbon dioxide passes from the blood into your lungs where it is then breathed out. It's an essential process, but it's also a system that is easily affected by stress.

As we've discussed, when your sympathetic nervous system is activated, it affects your breathing rate by increasing it significantly. This rapid breathing can cause you to become light-headed, and those same strong emotions can also result in shortness of breath. Additionally, if you have any preexisting respiratory problems like asthma or chronic obstructive pulmonary disease (COPD), the increased breathing rate can cause problems. Moreover, acute stressors, such as might occur when you get news of a disaster, can trigger an asthma attack, and the rapid breathing--also known as hyperventilation--can result in a panic attack.

Cardiovascular System

This is the system that includes your heart and your blood vessels. These work together to provide nutrients and oxygen to all of the organs and cells of the body. Again, it's another vital system. This system is also one of the principal responders in the event of stress. Acute stress results in an increased heart rate as well as stronger contractions of the heart muscles. Stress hormones like adrenaline and cortisol are what initiate these effects.

Those hormones also cause your blood vessels to dilate so they can better provide the necessary elements to the various parts of your body to help it respond adequately to the stressful situation. As the heart rate and volume of blood being pumped through your blood vessels increase, this causes your blood pressure to rise. With an acute stressor, everything goes back to normal after the problem is resolved.

A situation of chronic stress, such as that created by doomscrolling, can create long-term problems for your heart and blood vessels. You can, for example, develop hypertension, suffer a heart attack, or have a stroke. Chronic stress also contributes to inflammation in the circulatory system, and this is particularly problematic in the coronary arteries. If they become blocked by an inflammatory process, the result is a heart attack. Finally, chronic stress and how you respond to stress can also cause an increase in bad cholesterol, which can lead to blockages in the coronary arteries as well as other arteries.

With respect to this risk factor, there appears to be a difference between men and women. Women who are postmenopausal have lower estrogen levels. Estrogen helps the blood vessels to respond better to stressful situations, and thus, postmenopausal women may be at greater risk for problems related to chronic stress.

Gastrointestinal System

Scientists are only now gaining a fuller understanding of just how important your gastrointestinal system is for your health. Many doctors refer to this as your second brain. It has millions of nerves that function independently even as they maintain a constant communication with the brain. It's also very responsive to stress.

Chronic stress, such as that generated by doomscrolling, can result in pain, bloating, and other types of discomfort in the gut. Because the bacteria in your gut also affect your brain's health, stress can also affect your ability to think clearly and the emotions you experience. That means that changes in gut bacteria caused by chronic stress can help perpetuate a bad mood. Stress that occurs early in life can also change the way your nervous system develops and how your body reacts to stress in general. That can set you up for a lifetime of problems with your gut.

When you're stressed, you tend to eat either much more or much less than you normally do. You might also drink more alcohol or use tobacco, and all of that can result in acid reflux, also known as heartburn. A combination of stress and exhaustion, something common in doomscrollers, increases the severity of heartburn pain. This can cause your esophagus to spasm, something that creates intense pain that is often mistaken for a heart attack. It can also make it hard to swallow food, and it can increase the amount of air you swallow which results in gassiness, bloating, and a lot of burping.

All that bloating can also affect your stomach. Stress makes you feel any stomach pain more intensely, and if severe enough, can result in vomiting. Moreover, stress results in an increase or decrease in appetite which can ultimately negatively affect your mood. It isn't true, however, that stress increases a production in acid or causes ulcers. Ulcers are actually caused by a bacterial infection. But stress can make any ulcers you have more painful.

Your stress will also be felt in your bowels. There are involuntary muscle contractions in the smooth muscles of the bowels, and these movements are called peristalsis. It's what keeps the food moving through your gut as it is broken down into useful nutrients. Stress can either speed that process up, which results in diarrhea, or it can slow it down, which results in constipation. Additionally, stress can cause muscle spasms which are quite painful. This can also affect your digestion, and it can affect vital nutrient absorption by the intestines. That can result in deficiencies as well as gas production.

What's more, chronic stress can make the barrier in the intestines weaker, and that can result in bacteria entering your blood. While this bacterium is often easily taken care of by your immune system, the constant inflammation associated with this problem can cause further symptoms. Additionally, if you have a chronic bowel disorder like irritable bowel syndrome or inflammatory bowel disease, stress can result in increased sensitivity in the gut nerves, changes in the bacteria present in the gut, and changes in how quickly the food moves through your system. It can also change the gut's immune response. All of that can make for some extremely uncomfortable symptoms.

Nervous System

We've discussed the role of the sympathetic nervous system in initiating your body's response to a stressful situation and the role of the parasympathetic nervous system in calming you down once the problem has been resolved. The actions of each are accomplished through a cascade of biological responses that result in the production of various hormones.

In addition to these actions on the body, both of these systems interact in a powerful way with your immune system. Chronic stress can, therefore, drain your body's defense systems including the immune system. This can make you more susceptible to illness. It can also result in problems throughout your body as the continuous activation of the nervous system damages other bodily systems such as those of the gastrointestinal or cardiovascular systems.

Reproductive System

There are different effects of chronic stress on the reproductive system for men and women. For men, the sympathetic nervous system causes arousal and produces testosterone. When chronic stress results in the overproduction of cortisol in the adrenal glands, it can affect the normal function of the male reproductive system. It can result in lower levels of testosterone as the constant overstimulation causes the system to become fatigued. That results in a decline in your sex drive, and it can also cause erectile dysfunction as well as impotence.

Chronic stress can result in lower sperm levels, and it can affect sperm maturation thereby causing difficulties with conception. In fact, research has shown that men who have experienced just as little as two stressful life events within one year have a lower percentage of motile sperm--that is, sperm that can move normally. They also had a lower percentage of normally shaped sperm. Finally, because chronic stress affects the immune system, men may become more prone to infections in their testes, prostate gland, or urethra, all of which can affect the normal function of the reproductive organs.

For women, chronic stress can affect menstruation in numerous ways. It can cause an absent or irregular menstrual cycle as well as more painful periods and variations in the length of your cycle. It can also result in a reduction of sexual desire since women are already juggling so many demands in the course of their lives. Add chronic stress caused from constant doomscrolling to the mix, and it's no wonder they might experience less desire.

Chronic stress can also affect a woman's ability to conceive, as well as the health of her pregnancy and the postpartum adjustment she experiences. Doomscrolling can lead to increased anxiety and depression, and both of those problems are prominent causes of pregnancy complications and problems in the postpartum period. Stress during pregnancy can negatively affect both fetal and childhood development, and it can even disrupt the bonding between mother and child in the months after delivery.

For women who experience premenstrual syndrome (PMS), chronic stress can make those symptoms worse. Increased sensitivity to pain can make symptoms like cramping more intense, and stress can also increase problems of fluid retention and bloating. Additionally, stress can create more intense mood swings as well as more severe bad moods that are associated with PMS.

For those women approaching or experiencing menopause, chronic stress can add to the normal anxiety, mood swings, and feelings of distress to make those emotions more intense. That can make it much more difficult to deal with the physical changes a woman is experiencing during this time. The emotional stress makes the physical symptoms worse. Symptoms like hot flashes can be both more intense and more numerous as a result of chronic stress.

Lastly, an increase in stress can exacerbate existing reproductive diseases as well as make women more susceptible to developing a disease of the reproductive system. Remember that stress negatively affects your immune system and that makes you more prone to developing a new problem. It also makes it more difficult for your body to fight off existing problems.

General Health

The hormones, like cortisol, which are produced in response to an acute stress are generally helpful for helping your body respond to the situation. They reduce inflammation and help regulate the immune system so it is ready to respond should an injury occur. But, with chronic stress, the communication between the immune system and that HPA axis that regulates the stress response is impaired. Without those open lines of communication between these systems, you are left more susceptible to many physical and mental problems such as chronic fatigue, metabolic disorders like diabetes and obesity, and disorders of the immune system.

In sum, doomscrolling results in increased anxiety and stress, and when that persists over the long term, it has serious physical and mental health consequences. Life presents enough challenges without the added stressors associated with obsessively scrolling for negative news. It takes a heavy physical and mental toll on your health, but that's not all. It also affects your social life. That's what we'll examine in the next chapter.

5

HOW IT AFFECTS YOUR SOCIAL LIFE

When we look at the evolution of our species, it becomes clear that being a member of a group was, and continues to be, vital for our survival and for thriving in a given environment. That evolutionary history has hardwired a profound need for us to connect with each other and to be accepted as part of at least one social group. We need that sense of belonging, and part of getting that is developing and maintaining relationships with other people. When those bonds are severed, we feel disconnected and despondent. For someone who is already experiencing an elevated level of anxiety and depression, those feelings are more severe.

Normally, we don't get a thumbs up or thumbs down rating of a social interaction, and that leaves the impact of our interactions up to our own perceptions of the event. If you experience a positive social inter-action, you feel more like you belong. If, however, you're depressed or anxious given what you perceive to be the state of the world from doomscrolling, this will affect your information processing biases in such a way as to skew your interpretations of a social interaction. You're far more likely to miss the cues of acceptance and belonging that might have been present in that interaction. That means you're more likely to view it as negative when that might not have been the case at all.

What's more, if you view a social interaction as negative, your depression will likely result in you attributing the negative outcome to yourself rather than any other participants. That will then affect your actions regarding future social events, and that means you will most likely be left with the perception that you don't belong. Research shows that depressed people have fewer intimate relationships. They also don't elicit as many positive or caring responses from others, but they do experience more negative, rejecting responses. That means they are actually inducing negative responses in others, which then results in rejection and a loss of what might be socially rewarding opportunities (Steger & Kashdan, 2009).

As you can imagine, if you've been doomscrolling before a social event, and you bring that negativity into your interactions, it can be off-putting to say the least. That's something that can definitely induce a negative response in those around you. You're, in essence, creating the difficult social situation, and thereby, engendering worse interactions. What's more, your heightened anxiety and depression as a result of what you've been exposing yourself to on your social media feeds, causes you to look for those negative responses and social stimuli. It's a cascade of social dysfunction. You bring your brooding mood to the party which causes those around you to respond negatively, and your brooding mood draws your attention to those negative responses, all of which makes you feel worse.

Although you're on the lookout for those negative responses, your reactivity to both positive and negative stimuli is actually dulled. That means that your responses to the mess you're creating are slow, and when someone reacts to you in a positive manner, you also have an impaired reaction to that. All of that means you don't adjust your behavior according to the circumstances. Your delayed or even inappropriate reactions just make the situation worse. As the saying goes, "every party has a pooper!"

Research has confirmed that people with depressive symptoms experience less intimacy and enjoyment, and they perceive themselves to be less influential in social interactions. They also experience less stability in their sense of well-being. If you're more depressed and anxious, it also skews your interpretations of social events. In numerous studies, depressed people reported more negative social interactions and they also had less of a sense of belonging in those interactions. When they experienced a negative social interaction, that also lessened their sense of well-being (Steger & Kashdan, 2009).

Steger and Kashdan also studied the effects of depression on your sense of cognitive well-being. This relates to your assessment of meaning in your life--your judgments about whether or not your life makes sense and has purpose, and your life satisfaction--the degree to which you judge the conditions of your life to be satisfying and in accordance with your expectations. The researchers found that your judgment of meaning in life and life satisfaction is significantly related to the presence of depressive symptoms. In other words, if you are more anxious or depressed, you are likely to more negatively judge the meaning in your life and your life satisfaction. They also found that the need to belong, and whether or not you judge yourself as belonging, determines how much you appreciate your life. People with depressive symptoms feel the need to belong more strongly than those without, and thus, when they judge that they do belong, they appreciate their lives more.

Steger and Kashdan also argue that depressive symptoms are a warning sign that you should direct your limited attention resources to your current situation in order to avoid the possibility of rejection by the people in your life. If you think about this in the context of doomscrolling, if you're constantly and obsessively scrolling through your social media feeds for negative news, and you find you're depressed, this is your body's way of telling you to pay attention to this situation and make changes to avoid social ostracization.

While low levels of depressive symptoms might help you actually adapt your behavior to maintain your relationships, as the situation progresses, the warning your body was giving you now turns into hypersensitivity which only leads to more distress and dysfunction. The more you are distressed, the more you react negatively, and the more you focus on perceived negative interactions as a sign of looming rejection. This engenders a profound fear that has evolutionary origins. Rejection for our ancestors could easily have meant death. That's not as true for us in our modern world, but it still *feels* like it is. The more you perceive you might be rejected, the more depressed and hypersensitive you become. It's a downward spiral that won't end well for you. So, how exactly does all of this affect your relationships?

Romantic Partners

There are a number of ways in which your depression can affect your romantic partner. As you focus your attention on doomscrolling and sink ever deeper into a sense of hopelessness, it can feel as though you have lost yourself. You might feel uninspired, lonely, and dejected. All of this is not just challenging for you, it's also difficult for those closest to you. It's exceedingly difficult for anyone to live with someone who is consistently unhappy. Everyone experiences ups and downs, particularly in a romantic relationship, but when you're generating your own unhappiness by seeking out negative news, you create more downs than ups. That's a problem for your romantic partner.

The general unhappiness you're experiencing often creates problems with intimacy. As a result, your sex life suffers. That intimacy is an important part of maintaining a successful romantic relationship. When you have an active, healthy sex life with your partner, both of you release oxytocin, which is a hormone that helps you bond to one another. It boosts trust and helps to reduce stress. Thus, not only are you missing out on the intimate bonding with your partner, you're also missing out a mood boosting hormone that intimacy produces.

It is clear that depression lowers your libido, and it also affects your ability to achieve orgasm. It can also create problems related to erectile dysfunction. All that will most certainly take a toll on your relationship. It can leave your partner feeling unattractive and unimportant. It can lessen your sense of being close to one another, and it can make you feel as though you can't trust the other person. In fact, it can tempt one of you to stray from your committed relationship.

Depression also takes a toll on other areas of your relationship with one another. You likely won't feel inspired or motivated to do much of anything. You feel listless, and of course, you don't want to socialize. It can also make it difficult for you to keep your job, and you won't want to engage in other hobbies you might have previously enjoyed. These effects can take a toll on your relationship as they impact your social life together, and they can even jeopardize your shared finances.

Your partner will likely have trouble figuring out what to do to help you. That can make them feel useless, and as a result, they might even lose hope for salvaging the relationship. They love you, and they want to help you, but they don't know how. The fact that you're continuing to engage in an activity that makes the situation worse is confusing and frustrating. It's easy to see how they will feel as though they are helpless to change the situation. While only you can truly change it, that sense of helplessness can drive your romantic partner even further away.

Your own frustrations can result in the temptation to act out. This is particularly true for men. Women who are experiencing depression tend toward feelings of guilt, sadness, and worthlessness, but men more frequently externalize their feelings. They often will take to drinking, using drugs, engaging in abusive behavior, being more irritable, and/or behaving in a reckless manner. As you can imagine, all of that takes a heavy toll on an intimate relationship.

Using drugs, drinking excessively, or gambling can jeopardize your freedom and your shared finances. Acting out by cheating on your partner can certainly destroy your relationship. Minimally, it will cause a state of distrust, lowered self-esteem, and feelings of resentment. Moreover, these behaviors have a tendency to shut off the lines of communication. People experiencing feelings of depression already tend to shut down, and this just makes it worse.

When you lose the feeling that you can confide in your intimate partner, it becomes a lonely world indeed. Your spouse might still be supporting you because they love you, but it's easy to lose perspective. You might tend to think that they won't be able to understand what's happening to you, and that can make it genuinely difficult to communicate with them. Without that ability to communicate, however, your relationship will have difficulty growing.

All of these tendencies can spell the end of your intimate relationship. What's perhaps most difficult to realize, however, is that the habit that's causing your anxiety and depression is something that you can choose to change. If you don't, the problems you might be experiencing in your closest relationships can seep into every part of your life.

Children

If you have children, your mood and view of the world are definitely shaping both their internal and external experiences. First, your depression and anxiety as a result of your doomscrolling habit changes the way you interact with your children. You're likely less emotional and expressive with them, and you also make less eye contact with them. That can tremendously impact their ability to make healthy attachments, particularly if this is occurring when they're very young.

Additionally, your mood affects the way you engage in parenting activities. For example, you might not be as lively or expressive when you're reading a storybook together. That affects the way they understand the world and engage with others. You also may be limiting your child's social networks as you limit your own. Since you don't feel like going anywhere or doing anything, you probably won't be taking your child out to do things either. That can also create lifelong consequences for your child since it affects their ability to interact with others. Socialization at an early age is fundamental to shaping your child's ability to make friends and engage in social events.

Finally, your own depression can create a wide range of problems for your child. If you don't bond with them and nurture them because you're obsessed, depressed, and anxious, that will affect their own ability to bond with others. Also, depressed parents are less likely to do the things they need to do to ensure their children are safe, like getting vaccinations or using a car seat. This begins to show early in the child's life. The children of parents who suffer from depression and anxiety don't do as well in school, they are more likely to have behavioral problems, and they are just generally less healthy. Thus, your habit has far-reaching effects on your family, and it also takes a toll on your friendships.

Friendships

We've discussed some of the ways that your doomscrolling habit and resulting anxiety and depression can affect your social relationships, but let's look at some specific behaviors. These can deeply impact your friendships and your relationship with other family members. It can truly leave you isolated. Here are a couple of ways it affects your behavior:

- **You Blow Off Plans**: When you're lost in doomscrolling abyss, it's easy to blow off the plans you made last week or last month with your friends. You might be too involved in your habit, or your depression may make it impossible to get it together and go. So, you just don't show up...again and again. Pretty soon, your friends stop inviting you.

- **You Lash Out**: Doomscrolling is frustrating and irritating. You're confronted with things beyond your control, and you're angry about that as well as what you think is happening in the world. The resulting anxiety and depression can make you not only think hurtful things about yourself, but also about those around you. What's more, you often don't just think of them, you say them. This can drive a wedge between you and your friends and family. It will definitely affect their desire to have you around.

- **You Become a Hermit**: As you alienate the people in your life, pretty soon you find yourself isolated. You haven't shown up to the events to which you've been invited, and when you did show up, you were not the nicest person to be around. Your friends come to think of you full of nothing but 'doom and gloom.' It's not the most attractive feature. So, people stop asking, and you find yourself all alone.

- **You Become Convinced You're Unlikeable**: Your friends have seemingly abandoned you, you might even have lost your spouse, and for that, you think there's just nothing to like about you. The depression and anxiety generated by your doomscrolling has left you feeling as though everything is terrible in the world, and your personal circumstances just seem to confirm those feelings. But remember you're seeing the world through a distorted lens. Not only are you subjecting yourself to an intense level of negativity, your body and brain are also undergoing physical changes that affect your perspective and your mood.

By now, you can see there are a number of negative consequences to doomscrolling. It can ruin your relationships, make you depressed and anxious, and leave you isolated and feeling abandoned. While we've defined doomscrolling, it still might be difficult to determine where the line is between obsessively exposing yourself to negative news and simply staying informed about what's going on in the world. It can be a fine line, but that's what we'll examine in the next chapter--how to tell if you're a doomscroller.

6

HOW DID WE GET HERE AND HOW TO TELL IF YOU'RE A DOOMSCROLLER

By this point in the book, you might be wondering how doomscrolling came to be a thing, and how it is different from simply staying informed about what's going on in the world around you. It helps to understand the evolution of doomscrolling in order to understand how you might have been drawn into your obsessive habit. It has its roots in the rise of cable television.

You might be too young to remember this, but not that long ago, there were only four or five TV channels. Moreover, the news came on at specified times, and otherwise the TV channels ran soap operas or children's shows or prime time TV series with the occasional movie thrown in at specific times. There was no internet, so the only other place to get your news was by reading the newspaper.

That's what people did. They read the newspaper in the morning, watched the evening news before bed, and in between those times, they were busy living their lives--working, engaging with friends, playing with their children, and so on. By the 1990s, however, things were starting to change.

With the advent of cable television, there were many more channels for people to watch. That meant that TV channels had to compete with numerous entertainment channels for viewers. So, the news started to become increasingly negative, because that draws people's attention. What's more, the inherent human condition is such that anything left uncertain is intolerable. Whenever something isn't clear, which happens a lot as stressful events are unfolding, people are driven by those old evolutionary forces to seek more information.

Before the advent of 24/7 cable news and later the internet, you could only get your information when the news came on or in the news-paper the next morning. There was no other choice. But in the modern age, choices abound, and of course, as we've discussed, even just 14 minutes of bad news can negatively affect your mood and repeated exposure can traumatize you to the extent that you may experience PTSD symptoms years after the event.

This became sadly evident following the September 11 terrorist attacks. Not only were the attacks broadcast repeatedly, but the news media also focused almost solely on them. For perhaps the first time, you didn't have to be close to where the event happened to be affected by it. By simply switching on the TV, you could be exposed again and again to what had happened. And people were hungry for more. Watching the planes slam into those buildings was almost mesmer-izing as people sought to wrap their minds around what had happened.

This kind of repetitive focus on bad news had happened before, but the news wasn't on 24/7 at that time. I remember when the space shuttle Challenger blew up shortly after launch. A friend of mine who happens to be a psychologist remarked at that time that they had been playing the news coverage of the event at her work. Of course, immediately after the shuttle blew, the news went live and preempted normal programming, so it was on all the time. My friend became annoyed at the constant replay of the disaster. She remarked, "I must have watched that launch 20 times and never once has it not blown up."

While doomscrolling wasn't around at that time, she was unknowingly commenting on that human condition of constantly seeking more information and more clarity. We have a need to understand what happened and how any danger can be avoided in the future. Fast forward to 2020, a really bad year for almost everyone, and not only is there 24/7 coverage of all the negative news--of which there was plenty--but you can also now seek information online. Enter doomscrolling.

In between the 1990s and 2020, the competition for new outlets has only grown. Not only is there so much competition that most newspapers have gone virtual to try to keep up, but simply just reporting the story won't get you the audience you need to stay in business. You need to grab people's attention by reporting the extremes, emphasizing the danger, and provoking a strong emotional response in your viewer/reader. So, the headlines are dramatized, and if the story itself doesn't live up to the drama of the headline, the reader/viewer will look elsewhere.

Politicization of the News

Responsible journalism, as it's taught in the classroom, should objectively report on events and observations without favoring one viewpoint over another. Just the facts ma'am as the fictional detective Joe Friday on the show *Dragnet* was so fond of saying. But, with the increased competition, various news organizations began to slant the news toward one viewpoint or another on the political spectrum.

This is likely due, at least in part, to the rise of wealthy media moguls who more and more have sought to use their wealth to shape the news. There has always been propaganda that was disguised as journalism, but for the most part, that was limited to a few subjects and publications. In the modern age, however, many if not most media outlets are biased and slant the news toward a particular viewpoint. If you're a Fox news viewer, you get a decidedly different viewpoint on the same story from that of a CNN viewer.

What's more, nowadays, many news consumers get all their information from online sources such as Facebook and Twitter. Online, they can exist almost wholly within their social media bubble. They receive only the news that they've previously shown an interest in, media that skews to and reinforces their existing beliefs. You don't just go down the rabbit hole, you build a house and get a job and live there--just you and the red queen. But what is the difference between being informed about the world around you and being obsessive in your doomscrolling habits?

How Do You Know You're Hooked?

Like any kind of addiction, doomscrolling can start out slow and build up to a true obsession. It's normal to want to be informed, and when something happens, it's also normal to want to understand what happened and how tragedy can be avoided in the future. But there's a difference between that and constantly re-traumatizing yourself as you endlessly seek new details of an event with which you've already been informed about. What are the signs you're hooked? Here's a few:

The need to scroll: One sign you've got a problem is that, as with any addiction, you need your fix. You need to wake up and immediately check your feeds to see what's happened while you were sleeping, to find out what's new. If you wonder if this is you, try going one morning without checking your media feeds when you first get up. Or you might also try limiting yourself to just checking your feeds once a day. If it feels like you can't do that, you might have a problem.

Remember that doomscrolling becomes a habit, just like a drug or alcohol habit. You've trained your brain to engage in a habit routine once it receives the cue. That cue might be your alarm going off in the morning or the lunch bell ringing. Your brain urges you, and it's really good at urging, to engage in that habit routine so that it can get the reward it seeks--a shot of dopamine when you've satisfied it by running that habit routine.

The problem is that your need for information is never satisfied. That ancient part of your brain that wants you to get clarity so that danger can be avoided never feels relieved by the information you gain, so it keeps on prompting you to look for more.

Information relevant to you: It's easy to convince yourself that you're simply trying to stay informed, but if you find that you're scrolling about events or information that has no relevance in your life or that's long since been resolved, you might have a problem. You might have watched the space shuttle blow up 25 times, but if you still feel the need to watch it blow up 25 more times, maybe you're doomscrolling. If the information you're seeking is just repetitive without any new insights, then you're just re-traumatizing yourself.

Likewise, if the information you're seeking is about something that poses no danger to you--you're too far away or you're not in the group of people who would be affected, for example--then you might be doomscrolling. Staying informed regarding what's happening in the world requires one or two exposures to the information, and beyond that, it, once again, becomes a case of re-traumatizing yourself.

It feels like you just can't stop: As with any other kind of addiction, if you feel like you can't stop, that's a sign that you've got a problem. The habit cue is a strong impetus to take up the routine, and it's not easy to stop. Added to that is the evolutionary hardwiring of your brain to look for danger. The two together are a strong lure, but there are other strong survival urges that you're able to control.

You need to eat to survive, but you can control how much, when, and what. Having sex is a strong evolutionary urge, but you can control who you have sex with and when. So, while the need to learn as much as you can about any perceived threats is a strong one, you should be able to control it. If you can't limit it or stop altogether, you've got a problem.

It interferes with your life: As with any addiction, this is a big red flag. If you can't get to work on time because you can't stop doomscrolling and get ready for work, it's interfering with your life. If your marriage is falling apart because you spend all your time glued to your social media feeds, that's a problem. If you've lost your friends, alienated your family, and/or been cited for driving while using your cell phone--all because of doomscrolling--you've got a problem.

It doesn't help: If you find that you continue to scroll even though the knowledge you're gaining isn't helpful, it doesn't make you feel better, or it doesn't offer any solutions, then you're doomscrolling. There's a point at which the pursuit of knowledge becomes a cage in and of itself. When you find that you can't seem to distinguish what it is you need to know and what's just unnecessary fluff, that could indicate you have a problem.

Think about it this way--if you watch something like a presidential debate, you'll see how for most debates, the news media usually initially reports it was a tie. When people start to protest that one candidate or the other won, however, the news media starts to change its reporting to reflect that assessment. This has happened numerous times over many past debates. If you watched the last debate and then became involved in the hubbub that followed as the prevailing opinion changed, you witnessed that all happening in real time. But were you any more informed?

The reality is you could have watched the debate, then tuned out until watching the news the following day by which time the perspective of who won would have worked itself out. You would have saved yourself an enormous amount of time and what was really wasted effort.

Your scrolling didn't change any minds; it didn't help. It just wasted your time. Moreover, who won the debate may be irrelevant with respect to which candidate will win your vote. You may have watched the debate to help you decide. In that case, what the candidates say may be helpful information, but the media perspective of who won the debate isn't. So, you watch the debate and forget the rest. If you can't do that, you might be a doomscroller.

The reality is that knowledge can give you a sense of power, control, or purpose, but much of what's on the internet where you're obsessively scrolling is junk. Still, most people nowadays consider their phone to be something that makes them feel more powerful and confident. Take it away, and that sense of security goes with it.

When you consume too much information, however, it becomes increasingly difficult to process it in a way that is genuinely helpful. It's more difficult to remember all the facts and make sense of new information and/or unfamiliar opinions. To really understand what you're taking in, you need some time to mentally process it, to elaborate on what you've learned. That often means talking with people around you to get their take on it.

Additionally, you want to test new ideas against what you already know, you want to know if the new information makes sense in light of other established facts. By testing the new information against the reality you already know and taking the time to understand what might logically follow from the new revelations, you can improve the quality and complexity of your thinking. This requires time and motivation, and that won't happen if you feel either panicked or overwhelmed, a common consequence of doomscrolling.

In other venues like academia and in the financial markets, research has shown that if you have too much information, your decision-making capacity gets worse. That's because you simply can't elaborate on (i.e., process) all the information you're receiving. This can cause you to stop reflecting on anything at all. That means you're no longer carefully considering the facts or integrating the new information into what you already know. Instead, you're passively absorbing the information while it raises your blood pressure, destroys your sense of control, heightens your anxiety, erodes your attention span, and makes you feel depressed about pretty much everything in the world and in your life.

This very result is what some people are looking for when they put information on social media. Politicians are a fitting example. Negative political ads aren't really about changing your vote. They're geared toward making you feel apathetic and disengaged so that you won't vote at all, and it works. When they feed too much information into the system, it confuses people, and the negativity fills potential voters with confusion and a gloomy outlook on the whole process. It's easy for them to think that it's better to just not participate in a rigged system. That kind of thinking and the strategy behind it was on full display in the 2020 elections.

The political information circulated was not the kind that would be helpful for deciding who will win your vote. There were many rumors, claims, and innuendo, and none of it was regarding what the candidates were proposing, but if you fell into the rumor trap, it would be easy to have become overwhelmed and think that it may be better to just opt out of the process. And, in reality that's what most politicians--regardless of party--are wanting. It's better to only have to convince 25 percent of eligible voters to vote for you than 75 percent.

Here's the point--you don't have to keep exposing yourself to the kind of information that leaves you feeling disempowered, frightened, overwhelmed, or confused. Re-traumatizing yourself is simply not the same thing as staying informed about the world around you. You do not have a duty to consume upsetting junk news, and even if you're consuming good, solid journalism, you don't need to keep consuming it after you've learned about the topics reported.

Too much information triggers and re-triggers the sympathetic nervous system and makes it harder for you to focus. It can also make you feel unmotivated, helpless, and hopeless. I know I did. Furthermore, the fear and despair that kind of news generates makes you much easier to manipulate. But you can make better choices about your media habits. You can be more careful and reflective about what you're consuming. You can determine the kinds of information that are helpful for understanding the problem better. You can make choices to consume media that helps you feel more competent so that you can make good decisions about the action to take.

You can also choose to avoid those media sources that make you feel terrified, hopeless, or paralyzed. You can ask yourself who might benefit if you feel that way. When you start to look at your own habits and make better choices, you may find that your habits change considerably. You might only read recaps of the news once a week or just review headlines for a set period once a day. You might focus on local news rather than online sources of information. You might even delete your Twitter account.

There are things you can do to protect your mental and physical health from obsessively doomscrolling. That doesn't mean you have to put your head in the sand and check out, but it may mean monitoring and controlling your information consumption. It might be as simple as reading articles in full rather than simply scanning headlines. Those are usually dramatized and taken out of context. When you read the full story, you might not feel as frightened or overwhelmed.

The reality is that controlling your doomscrolling habit, like any other addiction, is about making better choices. It's also about bringing balance back into your life. In the next chapter, we'll explore some effective strategies for getting your media consumption habits under control. These strategies will help you find that balance you seek in your life.

7

HOW TO STOP DOOMSCROLLING

J ust like any bad habit, stopping means first acknowledging that you have a problem. It's only when you realize that your doom-scrolling is negatively affecting your life that you can effectively strategize to kick the habit. Toward that end, the first step to stop doomscrolling is to recognize just how bad your habit is, and you do that by documenting it thoroughly.

STEP #1: DOCUMENT YOUR HABIT

To document your habit, you start with observation. Get yourself a notebook and carry it with you everywhere. Don't try to change anything just yet, instead document it. Every time you start scrolling your social media feeds or obsessively watching news, take out your notebook and document the following information:

- The time--when you do it
- The location--where you do it
- What media you watched or read--be specific
- What you were thinking before you started scrolling
- What you were feeling before, during, and after scrolling
- Who you were with or if you were alone
- What you read about or watched
- Did you read the entire article or watch the entire report or just a snippet--document how much you read or watched
- What new information you learned about the topic you watched or read about
- How you felt about the information you read or watched

This will allow you to see the patterns involved in your habit. For example, I noticed that I would pick up my phone immediately when I woke up and start scrolling through my social media feeds. I would scroll some more as I ate breakfast, often ignoring my family as I did so. Every break I had at work, I scrolled, and when I got home in the evening, I would sit down and scroll some more. If I was watching TV, I would scroll when a commercial came on or if I felt the show was boring.

When I documented my habit, the first thing that struck me was just much time I wasted scrolling through my social media feeds. When I added it all up, it amounted to almost every free moment I had. It didn't seem like I was doing it that much when I was doing it, but it really adds up. I also found that it was something I turned to anytime I felt bored. Some people eat when they're bored, I doomscrolled. I also began to notice that I felt absolutely thrilled when I would hear about something dramatic that had happened and be the first to tell other people. It was like I had won some kind of prize for being the first to know among my friends.

I also noticed just how bad the news I was scrolling was and how negative it made me feel. There were many times when I was having a good day and feeling good until I started scrolling. I noticed a distinct change in my mood after reading negative headlines. And I noticed that was all I tended to read. Every now and again, a headline would prompt me to read more, but I almost never read the entire article. I read just enough to get the juicy details, but not enough to really understand the context in which they occurred. That was pretty shocking to me. I had always justified my habit with the thought that I was a modern, well-informed, and responsible citizen. The reality, however, was that I was just a headline hound. I knew very little beyond what that overly dramatized snippet of information had to offer.

This exercise was a real eye-opener for me. I hadn't expected to find out what I did. I guess a part of me thought that I would find I was, in fact, justified in my habit, that I was just keeping myself informed. Boy, was I in for a shock. When I started changing my habit, I really began to learn just how much I was missing by doomscrolling.

STEP #2: ONE STEP AT A TIME

Whenever you're changing a habit routine, you're working against some very well-established and powerful networks in your brain. Normally, establishing habit routines are helpful to us. They free our mind to work on other things while we engage in tasks that don't take much mental concentration.

For example, brushing your teeth is a habit routine you engage in every day. When you were first learning to brush your teeth, you had to concentrate, and you had to remember to do it each day at certain times. But, once you get the routine down, it becomes almost automatic. You no longer have to concentrate while you put toothpaste on your toothbrush or move the brush around your mouth.

You've actually got a lot of habit routines that you engage in every day. You brush your teeth, shower, buckle your seatbelt when you get in the car, and drive the same route to work. While you pay attention as you're driving, you don't have to concentrate on the driving itself. Once it's a habit, you do it without having to think about it. If you ever have the chance to drive in a country where they drive on the other side of the road, you'll see just how much of a habit driving has become!

What happens in the brain as you're making something into a habit is a big part of the reason why it's difficult to change. First, the brain sends signals to specific parts of the brain. Then, specialized neurons (nerve cells) in the brain begin to fire. These cells prompt you to initiate the habit routine after picking up on the cue, they prevent another habit routine from running simultaneously, and they mark the end of the habit routine.

The pathways of communication between various areas of the brain and your body are strengthened each time you engage in the habit routine. It's like walking down the same path in the forest every day.

The path becomes clearer and more well-established the more you walk down it. Once this path is clearly established, it would be difficult to take another route.

Erasing the pathways is difficult as is ignoring the urges when your brain prompts you to engage in the habit routine. But there is a technique you can use to simply replace the bad habit with something good. That way you don't have to erase the pathways, you can use the same pathways, but just change the habit routine.

Habit Stacking

Habit stacking is a process whereby you stack a new, good habit on top of an existing habit routine. You do this all the time in your normal life. You brush your teeth and then hop in the shower. Those are two habit routines that are commonly stacked. You do one and then the other. The remarkable thing about habit stacking is that you can use those well-worn paths in your brain to just insert a new, better behavior, but you want to do it in stages.

It takes anywhere from 22 to 90 days to establish a new routine in such a way that you no longer need to think about doing it. That's the first thing to realize: you will have to make an effort at first, but once you've successfully kept up with the new routine for a period of time, your brain will start prompting you to engage in the new routine instead of the old one. Here are some tips for starting slow and building to an entirely new routine:

Start small: The key here is that you don't want to jump into a big change immediately. If you're like I was, you reach for your phone immediately upon waking up. So, begin changing your doomscrolling habits by waiting simply five minutes before picking up that phone. Do that for a week, and then you can increase in the time to ten minutes. Do that for another week or two, and you're ready for the next change.

Don't use your phone as an alarm and place your phone away from your bed: By now, you're accustomed to waiting a little before reaching for your phone, by moving it away from your bed, you now put another change that requires more effort to start doomscrolling. Do this for two weeks before moving on to the next step.

Engage in another routine before scrolling: Now, you want to institute another short routine into your scrolling time. You might decide, for example, to spend just three minutes meditating before picking up the phone to start scrolling. Perhaps, you'll make a commitment to do 10 jumping jacks before reaching for the phone or two yoga stretches.

Whatever you do, keep it simple and short, and do it every time you are wanting to reach for your phone to start scrolling. The key to picking up new, better habits is making it easy to do and fast. If it is too difficult or takes too long, you won't stick to it. Again, do this for one to two weeks before moving on to the next phase.

Set a time limit for your scrolling: You're beginning to change your morning routine of doomscrolling, but this next phase can apply to all of your habitual times for scrolling your news feeds. Set a strict time limit--maybe just five or ten minutes --using your phone's alarm, and when the alarm goes off, set your phone down without looking at it any further. Do this for one to two weeks before instituting the next step.

Put your phone someplace else: By now, you've instituted another routine before you begin scrolling, you wait to scroll when you feel the urge, and you set a time limit for your scrolling. By placing your phone away from where you are, it will make it more difficult for you to pick it up and start scrolling. It will make your scrolling intentional rather than automatic.

If you're at work, place your phone in the glove compartment of your car (be sure to lock your car), and if you're at home relaxing, place your phone in another room from where you're sitting. That means you have to make the decision to get up and go get your phone to start scrolling. But, before you do that, wait that five or ten minutes and engage in the meditation (or other) routine. Then, if you do pick up your phone, stick to the time limit you've set. Do this for another one to two weeks.

Replace doomscrolling with something that creates joy for all but two scrolling times per day: Now, you're ready to cut down on the actual doomscrolling that you do. Establish just two times in the day when you will allow yourself to scroll your social media feeds. During the other times that you would normally be scrolling, replace that activity with something that brings you joy. You might, for example, be a fan of crossword puzzles or maybe you like poetry. It's even better if it is something uplifting, but it can also just be fun. When you get the desire to scroll, wait the pre-established length of time, engage in your short meditation or exercise routine, and then instead of picking up your phone, do a crossword puzzle, read an inspiring poem, or engage in whatever other joyful activity you've chosen to replace your doomscrolling habit.

Cut it down to once a day: After a few weeks of only allowing yourself to scroll your social media feeds twice a day, cut it down to one time a day and limit that time to no more than 15 or 20 minutes. You can also choose to consume your news in another way, like by watching your local news instead of doomscrolling. That can help you eliminate the habit altogether.

STEP #3: MORE CHANGES TO SUPPORT YOUR NEW HABITS

There are a number of other things you can now do to support your new good habit and ensure you don't slip back into doomscrolling. The first thing to do is opt out of news alerts. That way you won't be tempted to check your feeds every time you hear that notification tone. As you're now consuming your news in an intentional manner rather than simply giving into the mindless repetition that characterizes doomscrolling.

Start spending more time doing things you enjoy. Now that you've got a large part of your life back, you can really start to enjoy other aspects of your life. Take a short walk outside on your break instead of reaching for your phone. Spend time at the gym or exercising outside after work or in the morning. Now that you're not spending all that time scrolling your social media feeds, you'll be able to really rebuild your life.

STEP #4: GIVE IT TIME

Establishing a new habit routine takes time. It's hard to create new boundaries around the use of your phone and your doomscrolling habit, but with time, you'll find your mood has improved and you have much more time to do other things. As you repeat the new, better habit routines you've used in place of doomscrolling, your brain will strengthen those pathways, and soon, you'll find it's urging you to engage in the new activities. Before you know it, you'll be reinventing your life. It's literally rewiring your mind, but that's something we'll explore in more detail in the next chapter.

8

REWIRING YOUR MIND

As we're talking about changing your habits, it's a good idea to understand just what's involved in the formation of habits and breaking them. It's relevant because this process literally involves rewiring your mind, and when you understand what's happening internally, you'll have more motivation to keep up the good work.

Your brain is a far more powerful organ that you might realize. Its function has been modified by millions of years of evolution, and its prime directive is to help you survive. Remember that your brain is on the job from the time you're born to the time you die. During that time, it's busy processing information to which you're exposed as well as the experiences you have in life. It also manages hundreds upon thousands of necessary involuntary functions, many of which are involved in habit formation.

Essentially, when categorizing your habits as good or bad, the reality is that it's a continuum, right? A mildly bad habit might be something like failing to pick up your dirty socks and put them in the laundry basket. A moderately bad habit could be getting tipsy at the office Christmas party and letting loose a little more than you should. A strong bad habit is something that can really damage your health, like smoking cigarettes.

Your habits are also on a continuum with regard to the level of control you can exert on the habit. Your mildly bad habits might be relatively easy to overcome but overcoming that addiction to tobacco is another story. Once a habit is deeply ingrained in your brain--i.e., those pathways are well-established--it will be much more difficult to exercise control over them. That's why you have to begin by documenting the behavior associated with the habit.

By documenting the patterns associated with your doomscrolling habit, you can see what triggers the behavior, and you can better understand the reward you get from engaging in the behavior. The reward behind most habits is a shot of the brain's feel-good chemical dopamine. This is something your brain produces that makes you feel good, and it's definitely addictive. Who doesn't want to feel good?

When you begin the process of documenting the behavioral patterns around your doomscrolling habits, you start to see the bigger picture. There may be other habits associated with doomscrolling. For example, it might be part of your work routine. You might get into work, doomscroll for the first 15 minutes of your day, then go get some coffee where you strike up a conversation with your best office friend about what you've just read while doomscrolling.

So, part of the doomscrolling habit is this larger routine that gives you not just the reward associated with the doomscrolling, but the social reward of chatting with your officemate about it. Changing your doomscrolling habit will likely affect the associated habits as well. That's something you'll want to prepare for so that you aren't lured back into your old ways.

It's important to get a handle on your bad habits, because they can literally damage your brain. Being overly attached to electronic devices is something that has a strong negative effect on the brain. It causes addiction, and too much internet can even damage your frontal lobe, as we've discussed previously. Specifically, there's a part of your brain called the striatum which helps control and suppress improper impulses. It also helps direct you to activities that are rewarding for you. When you engage in addictive electronic habits like doom-scrolling, you reduce the brain's cortical thickness which results in cognitive impairment. Let's look at how this happens as you form patterns.

Habits and Habit Formation

You probably don't realize it, but habits actually comprise some 40 percent of your daily behavioral patterns. As previously mentioned, that can be a good thing since it frees your brain for doing other things as you engage in specific repetitive behaviors like brushing your teeth. That's helpful given that there are many repetitive routines that don't require constant conscious thought to complete successfully. But how do habits, good or bad, form?

Basically, when you form a habit, you train your brain to respond to a specific cue by initiating a habit routine that, when complete, results in a reward for your brain. Remember, your brain is constantly scanning your environment on the lookout for threats and hungry for rewards. When you engage in repetitive habitual behavior, you're giving your brain that chemical reward in the form of dopamine, and that makes your brain hungry for even more. The basis for habit formation can be put into two categories: psychological or physiological.

Psychological Habits

These are habits that form as part of a mechanism for learning. In other words, you make certain acceptable internal decisions, and as you learn from the experiences that follow from those internal decisions, you retain that knowledge either consciously or subconsciously. If you are retaining the lesson and repeating the experience, the acquired disposition that results becomes a habit. For example, if you learn that smiling at your partner and giving him or her a kiss when they come through the door puts them in a good mood, that behavior becomes a habit that you do automatically. Likewise, if you learn that yelling at an underling at work gets them to do the job faster which reflects well on you, that becomes a habit.

Physiological Habit Formation

This type of habit formation involves your nervous system. By repeating an action over time, you're building up a nervous system pathway which then directs certain electrical stimuli to specific receptors in the brain, and that results in the stimulation of certain behaviors. There are specific neurons that mark both the beginning and end of a habit routine, and there are different neurons that keep another habit routine from running at the same time. As you engage more and more in this habit routine, that pathway--just like the path through the forest--becomes strengthened.

These are the two ways that habits form, but there are a number of different types of habits as well, some of which are conscious and some of which are unconscious.

Unconscious Habits

These are habits that are reflexive kinds of functions that you do without any thought. These are things like physical and mental activities that you likely would never describe as habits. These can determine your values, emotions, creativity, personality, and cognitive prejudices among other things. They can be characterized as motor habits, intellectual habits, and habits of character.

Motor habits are those that involve muscular actions like sitting, standing, or walking. As you move, your brain stores the information as part of a habit routine. These involve the work of both your cerebrum (the part of your brain that controls your thoughts and conscious movement) and your cerebellum, the part of your brain that controls those kinds of activities you have no conscious awareness of like digesting your food, breathing, and your reflexes. When you move in certain habitual ways, your cerebrum tells your cerebellum to store that motion as a learned reflex, or a habit.

Intellectual habits are those that engage your intellectual abilities as well as your psychological processes. As you use reason to make decisions, you apply logic to your thoughts. The more you engage in this kind of analysis, the stronger your intellectual habits become. They become similar to a reflex in that you simply engage in a repetitive manner of gaining knowledge and analyzing it. These kinds of habits keep you from having to ponder or hesitate when deciding certain things like which hand to use when you write. It is your intellectual habits that can be undermined by the sheer volume of information you're exposed to with doomscrolling. When you are unable to apply the normal habit routines associated with intellectual assessment of the information to which you're exposed, it can cause you to quit trying.

The last type of unconscious habits is those of character. These include things like your work ethic, your ability to manage your time efficiently, your consideration for family and friends, your empathy, or even the fact that you tend to trust people when you first meet them. These kinds of habits require two steps: first, you embrace a virtue like honesty, and second, you set up and cultivate habits that reinforce the virtue. You perceive the merits of honesty as the reward for your efforts. After repeatedly being honest, and being rewarded for that honesty, it simply becomes automatic, a habit. This too, can be undermined by doomscrolling. Being repeatedly exposed to unreliable information that undermines your intellectual habits can cause you to adopt less virtuous habits as you attempt to formulate responses to perceived threats. If you believe the conspiracy theories you're reading about, for example, you might decide to engage in less virtuous behavior to respond to them.

Conscious Habits

These are habits that are associated with conscious habits like doom-scrolling. These kinds of habits require critical thinking, decision-making, planning, judgment, short-term memory, and willpower. As with unconscious habits, there are different kinds of conscious habits.

Keystone habits are those that have a kind of domino effect and impact many different areas of your life. These habits underlie other habits. So, for example, if your doomscrolling habit causes you to then develop a habit of being late to work or avoiding certain social situations, it's a keystone habit. These can be positive too--your habitual exercise routine helps you get a good night's sleep and prompts you to engage in healthier eating habits.

Support habits are those unintentional habits that result from your keystone habit. So, you develop that habit of being late to work unintentionally as a result of your intentional doomscrolling keystone habit. The late work habit is a support habit developed as a result of the doomscrolling.

The final type of conscious habit is an elephant habit. These habits require more time to form. An example would be if you develop a habit of cleaning out one part of your house each day as your work toward an overall goal of cleaning the whole thing. It relates to the old joke; how do you eat an elephant? One bite at a time. If you have a huge task, developing these little habits to get it done helps you achieve your goal. The little, consistent habits that work toward the larger goal make a huge difference over time. Regarding your doom-scrolling habit, these are the slight adjustments we discussed in the previous chapter. As you make small changes to your habit routine, those work toward helping you curb your overall goal of kicking your doomscrolling habit.

That's the genius of implementing the tiny habits we discussed in the last chapter. They are so ridiculously easy to implement that there's no reason not to do them. You can't yet kick the morning doomscrolling habit altogether, but you can wait five tiny minutes after you wake up to start doing it. Then, you implement another tiny, elephant habit--I know that's an oxymoron, but it works. Those incremental changes add up faster than you think they will.

As you build these small habits to a larger scale, you now have stacked new, better habits onto that already well-worn pathway in your brain. That's why habit stacking is so effective. It rewires your brain to trigger a different, better habit using the same cues and the same rewards. But there's one more part to this--synaptic pruning.

Synaptic Pruning

This is a phenomenon that occurs in everyone with age. It involves the connections between neurons in your brain. But first a little vocabulary and anatomy lesson. A synapse is a gap between neurons (nerve cells). Electrical messengers in your brain run along the nerve cells, but then they come to this gap. They have to jump the gap. To link one neuron to another and form that strong pathway in your brain, you've got to have a way to jump the gap. That's where many of the brain's neurochemicals come in. They jump the gap so that the electrical stimulus can continue along its way.

When you repeatedly engage in a certain habitual behavior, your brain stores and builds up those frequently used neurons and synapses. It also prunes the neurons and synapses that don't get used over time. So, when you learned to play the piano as a child, your brain created numerous neurons and synapses, and each time you practice, those pathways are strengthened. They become more efficient and faster as well as stronger as you practice, and that helps you play better. If you also experimented with playing the drums, but never went on to develop that skill, then the neurons associated with that skill will be pruned.

This process actually explains why the brains of newborn babies have 41 percent more neurons than that brain of the average adult. There's a whole world of possibilities in the newborn brain, and when that child begins to engage in habitual behaviors favoring certain skills over others, the unused neurons and synapses will be pruned (Abitz et al., 2007). While they have more neurons, the pathways are not strongly developed in their brains. That takes repetitive behaviors.

What this means for your doomscrolling habit is that, as you begin to replace that bad habit with better habits, you'll engage less in the doomscrolling. If you're able to kick the habit altogether, eventually those neurons and synapses related to the doomscrolling habit routine will be pruned. This will just help you to make your new habits even stronger. Remember that your brain is stimulated to deal with what's happening now, not what's happened in the past or what might happen in the future. Thus, as you strengthen the pathways for new habits, it will respond by clearing out the old clutter.

So, this is how introducing new habits into your old routines can help you to rewire your brain as you kick the doomscrolling habit. But there are other effects of your habit that need some work too. I know that when I was doomscrolling, I stopped exercising and I didn't care about eating right. That meant I had some work to do to get my body back in shape after I quit the habit. That's what we'll explore in the next chapter--retuning your body.

9

RETUNING YOUR BODY

When I began to entrench myself more deeply into my doomscrolling habit during the quarantines of the 2020 pandemic, one of the first things that happened was that I stopped exercising. I was left without any motivation because of the depression and anxiety I felt. The more I doomscrolled, the worse I felt, and the more I neglected my physical health, the worse I felt. It was just all bad news. That was just another good reason for quitting the doomscrolling habit, but once I had stopped, I realized I had to get back into shape.

If you've ever needed to get back into shape, you know it can be a challenge just to get that motivation back. You'll be amazed, however, how once you stop the constant influx of negative information and the emotions that causes, you'll find that your energy levels soar. It will be much easier to find that motivation to get back into a healthy exercise routine. Before we talk about doing that, let's look at just what neglecting your body does to your health. These are part of the physical side effects of your doomscrolling habit.

Blood Pressure

Your blood pressure soars, and this is something that happens almost immediately when you quit exercising. In fact, if you're engaging in a normal exercise routine, your blood pressure rises on those days when you don't exercise. So, if just one day of rest from a routine can cause that kind of effect, you can imagine what stopping altogether does. After two weeks of no exercise, your blood vessels begin to adapt to the new normal and that further increases your blood pressure. After one month, your arteries and veins begin to stiffen to the point where your blood pressure rises to where it would be if you had never worked out in your life. It will take a month or two of routine workouts to get it back down to where your blood vessels are functioning efficiently again.

Muscles

Believe it or not, just three days of missed workouts results in measurable changes in your body. One of those changes is that your muscles begin to shrink. As your muscle mass decreases, muscle fibers start to lose their ability to burn fat. Of course, you will also begin to lose the strength your workouts helped give you. This isn't something you'll see so much when you look in the mirror, but when you go back to the gym or resume other activities, you'll notice the difference. Your muscles will become fatigued much faster than when you were working out regularly. Of course, those muscles that you don't use much during daily activities will lose their tone the fastest. These are muscles such as those in your abdomen. And, when you do see a difference in the mirror, it's these muscles that will show that first.

Endurance

Your endurance refers to the amount of time it takes for you to become fatigued when engaging in activity, and a decrease in endurance also happens very quickly when you quit working out. In fact, within two weeks of stopping your workouts, the amount of oxygen your body takes in and uses drops by 10 percent. This makes it harder for you to do almost everything in your life that requires physical activity. That can have profound effects on your life quality. If you have kids, it will become much harder to keep up with them, and even if not, just engaging with your friends and family in relatively easy activities will become much harder. That will just add to your sense of isolation.

Bones

You might not think about your bones when you quit working out, but they will become weaker as a result. This isn't a change you will see in the mirror, but within a year of stopping your exercise routine, your bones will be measurably weaker. Without weight bearing activities, the bones become brittle. This puts you at risk--men and women--of osteoporosis. That's right, it's not just for older women, it can happen for other reasons too. You see, your muscles attach to your bones, and in fact, your muscles are what allows you to move your bones. As you use your muscles to work out, they pull on the bone, and in response, the bone builds itself up so it can withstand the force the muscles are exerting on it. That's why anywhere a muscle attaches to a bone, there's a ridge. The more you work out, the bigger those ridges become. That helps keep your bones strong.

Body Weight

Within just five weeks of quitting your workout routine, you'll see a measurable increase in body fat. If you don't alter your diet, you'll definitely gain weight. That's the only way you can avoid weight gain, but I know that the deeper I got into doomscrolling, the worse my eating habits became. Depression and anxiety are not a good emotional state for healthy eating, so that makes it difficult to eat better if you're not working out.

Blood Sugar

This is yet another change that happens very quickly after you quit working out. In fact, your blood sugar will rise after only five days of quitting your workout routine. Your blood sugar normally rises after you've eaten, and then, it drops again as your body begins absorbing the sugar you've eaten and turning it into energy. When you quit working out, however, the elevated blood sugar levels you experience following a meal will stay elevated instead of dropping. When you continuously have elevated blood sugar levels, you increase your risk of diabetes and heart disease. The good news is that after just a week of getting back into a regular exercise routine, your blood sugar levels will drop dramatically.

Mood

We've discussed at length how doomscrolling affects your mood just because of the negative information you're consuming. This is compounded by quitting your regular exercise routine. Exercise causes your brain to produce endorphins. Those are the brain's feel-good chemicals, and the result is that you feel better following a workout. When you quit working out, your brain isn't producing as much of those chemicals, and that can just add to the depression and anxiety you're feeling as a result of the doomscrolling. But you'll also start to feel worse as your appearance changes because you're no longer working out. In short, your mood will just keep getting worse.

Brain Functions

Just as you rewire your brain when you change a habit, you also change your brain when you stop exercising. After just ten days without exercise, the blood flow to various areas of your brain that involve higher thought processes and memory will decrease. That means your cognitive abilities will take a hit as you become less active.

Joints

Along with everything else, stopping an exercise routine means your joints will ache more. This is particularly true if you're older. What happens is that your ligaments and cartilage that support your joints are affected when you quit working out. What's more, recovering their function takes longer than other parts of the body. These tissues--tendons, ligaments, and cartilage--have less blood flow than other tissues, so that affects their ability to recover when you start working out again.

Fitness Goals

Once you've stopped working out, you'll have to start over at square one to get back to your previous fitness goals. You'll have to start at the beginning again, but it is worth doing, and you can get back on track toward the same goals you had previously. You just have to start out at lower intensities and build back up to where you were before. That will take about six weeks, but from there you can start increasing the number, intensity, and time for your workouts.

Tips for Getting Back to It

With a full understanding of how stopping your workout routine affects your body, it's important to emphasize that it's worth the effort to get back to it. It's not an uncommon situation to be in. Many people get off track with their fitness at one time or another in their lives. You can get it back, but there is a right way and a wrong way to do it. These tips are designed to help you do it the right way so that you won't suffer an injury and you will reach your new fitness goals.

1. **Get Moving**: The important thing to do when you're trying to get back into a workout routine is to get moving. That means do anything you're able to do. You might have to start with simple exercises or a shortened time frame for working out. That's okay, just get moving. It's best to train your entire body, but if you want to just start with walking or an upper body routine or even just one arm, it's something. It gets you started and helps you move on to other exercises that eventually will work out your entire body.

2. **Quality in Motion**: You want to get moving, but it needs to be motion that is done normally with good technique. Good technique is better than speed or repetition. If you need to slow down to ensure you're doing the movements properly, then that's what you should do. It doesn't really matter how slowly you need to start; you'll be able to pick up speed over time. Just don't expect too much too soon. If you push yourself to do something fast but with bad technique, you'll be defeating the purpose of the workout.

3. **Eat Protein**: When you've been inactive, your protein requirements increase. That's because how your body metabolizes protein shifts to the protein metabolism of an older person. That means it's a lower efficiency metabolism that requires more protein to achieve the same results. As you get back into an exercise routine, you'll need more protein to keep up with your daily maintenance. Essentially, you'll want to eat one gram of protein per pound of lean body mass. There are a number of additive protein sources like whey that you can use to boost your protein intake.

4. **Pain versus Soreness**: As you get back to working out, it's important to listen to your body. You want to avoid pain, but it's likely you'll experience soreness. Soreness is normal and it indicates your muscles are working. Pain, however, is something else, and that can indicate an injury. Soreness tends to be a dull achy sensation whereas pain tends to be sharp. Soreness may last for a day or two, but pain typically lasts for days. If you feel pain, you should stop the workout and seek medical attention. To avoid

injury, it's important to be aware of what your body is telling you.

5. **Walking**: Regular walking is a terrific way to get back in the game. It tells your body that you're engaged with the world and you're back at it. It's a simple, fundamental way to get that blood flowing, lubricate your joints, and stimulate your musculoskeletal system. What's more, most everyone can do it. It's helpful to utilize any hills in your area to help you take it up a notch as you're walking. Walking up and down those hills can help build up your strength and endurance. You can also wear a weighted vest, leg weights, or even just put some books in a backpack so that you can add some resistance to your workout. If you can work up to five times of walking per week for 30 to 45 minutes, this is a great way to get moving again.

6. **Bear Crawls**: These are a great way to loosen your joints and get your shoulders ready for more difficult movements. It's a great way to get back into working out. These can be done several times each week in the morning or before your workout for just a few minutes. Crawl forward, backward, and then go side to side, but make sure you really feel the movements.

7. **Balance Work**: This helps you prepare for more complex movements and it tones the muscles you use to keep your balance. A basic balance exercise is just to stand on one foot while slowly sweeping the other foot in front of you and behind you. Repeat on the other side. Do this just a few minutes every day or even if you have just a few moments of

down time like when you're standing in line. Another good balance exercise involves placing a 2 X 4 on the ground and then you walk forward and backward along the board. You're balancing on a narrow surface, but there's no risk if you fall off. Again, do this for a few minutes each day.

8. **Bodyweight Exercises**: These are exercises you do where you're simply manipulating your own body weight without using external weights. These include basic movements like squats, lunges, pushups, triceps dips, etc. You want to include these in your workout routine since they're a great way to get into weight training that does use external weights, and they really help to build your muscle tone and strengthen your bones. By starting your exercise regimen with bodyweight exercises, you also warm your body up for more complex or difficult exercises. This is critical to your routine, and it's a great starting point after you've been idle for a while.

9. **End with Bodyweight Exercises**: Beginning with bodyweight exercises are a great way to warm your body up and ending with bodyweight exercises are a great way to cool down. These types of exercises are great for building strength and general fitness. By sandwiching your cardio exercises with bodyweight exercises, you'll find your body will respond more quickly to the workout regimen and you'll better protect yourself from injury.

10. **Include Fish Oil or Fatty Fish in Your Diet**: Fatty fish or fish oil are a great source of high-quality protein that can help to supply your body with what you need to get back

into your exercise routine. But fatty fish and fish oil are also a great source of long chain omega-3 fatty acids. These are potent anti-inflammatory effects that help speed your return to a normal active routine. That will help to reduce any pain you experience as you get back into your exercise regimen. In fact, high dose omega-3 fatty acids can help you increase physical activity, maintain proper physical function, and decrease the need for a joint replacement as you grow older. The last benefit of omega-3 fatty acids is that they increase muscle protein synthesis. That means they help you build muscle back that you've lost after being inactive, and they do that by making your physical activity more anabolic.

SAMPLE EXERCISE ROUTINES

Now that we've examined the problems associated with inactivity and a few tips to use as you get back into an exercise routine, let's look at two different possible routines you can use to get moving again. These incorporate the tips listed above as well as a few other movements that are helpful for beginning again.

Exercise Routine #1

For this routine, there are three workouts. Each of the workouts should be done once per week with a day of rest in between each. Those exercises marked with "A" and "B" indicate that you should do a set of A's first, then rest, then do a set of B, and rest again. Then, repeat. The warmup should be used for each of the three workouts.

Several exercises are also assigned a specific tempo. The first number is the time in seconds that you should be using to do the movement, the second number is the time you should pause at the full extension of the movement, the third number is the time for returning to the start position, and the fourth number is how long you should pause before going again. A "0" indicates no time, and an "X" means that movement should be performed explosively. As an example, if you're doing an ab rollout and the tempo is 4-3-X-0, that means you should take 4 seconds to roll the wheel out until your body is fully extended, hold that position for 3 seconds, come back fast (explosively), and then begin the next rollout immediately without any pause.

Warmup

1. Epic Stretch

Sets: 1
Reps: 3 on each side
Rest: 0 seconds

Begin in a deep lunge position such that your front thigh is parallel to the floor and your back leg is straight. Twist your torso toward the side of your front leg and reach your hand on that side up over your head.

2. Inchworm, inchworm...

Sets: 1

Reps: 3

Rest: 0 seconds

Bend at the waist and place your hands on the floor in front of you. Walk your hands out so that your torso straightens out and you end up in the plank position with your hands under your shoulders. Now, walk your hands out further. As you're in this position, don't allow your hips to sag--keep your abdomen taut. Then walk your hands back and return to a standing position.

3. Wall Slide

Sets: 1

Reps: 10

Rest: 0 seconds

Place your back against a wall and raise your arms above your head with the backs of your hands against the wall. Keep contact with the wall as you draw your elbows to your sides.

4. Mini Band Side Step

Sets: 1

Reps: 15 on each side

Rest: 0 seconds

Take a small band and loop it around your ankles. Bend your hips and knees so that you are in a half squat position. Take one small step to the left so that there is tension on the band. Then, walk sideways keeping the band taut for 15 steps to the left. Repeat going to the right side so that you return to where you started.

Once you're warmed up, it's time to start the workout. Let's start with day number one. For these exercises, you'll need weight training equipment. If you are unfamiliar with the equipment described, please ask a trainer or employee of your gym to help you out. You should always choose a weight you feel comfortable lifting. While you can gradually increase that weight, if in doubt, start with less weight.

Day 1 Workout

1. A. Front Squat

Sets: 4

Reps: 8

Tempo: 4-0-X-0

Rest: 60 seconds

Grasp the weight bar with your hands shoulder width apart. Raise your elbows out in front of you so that your upper arms are parallel with the floor. Lift the weight bar out of the rack and let it come to a rest on your fingertips. Your hands are palms up with your fingers pointed back toward your shoulders. The bar is resting on your fingers. Step back so that your feet are shoulder-width apart and your toes are turned out slightly. Squat down while maintaining the arch in your lower back.

1. B. Neutral Grip Pullup

Sets: 4

Reps: 8

Tempo: 4-0-X-0

Rest: 60 seconds

This requires a chin up bar that has handles where you can pull yourself up as your palms are facing each other. If you just have a straight bar, you can hook a V-grip cable handle over it. Grab the bar with your palms facing each other and pull yourself up until your chin is above the bar.

2. A. Ab Rollout

Sets: 4

Reps: 8

Tempo: 4-0-X-0

Rest: 60 seconds

Using an ab wheel or a bar with 10-pound plates, position yourself with your shoulders over the wheel (or over the bar). Contract your abs and roll forward until you feel as though your hips will sag. Then, roll yourself back to the starting position.

2. B. T-Bar Row

Sets: 4

Reps: 8

Rest: 60 seconds

Use either a T-bar row station or wedge a barbell into a corner and then attach a V-grip handle under it. Straddle the bar and with your lower back arched, bend forward at the hips so that your torso is almost parallel with the floor. Grasp the T-bar or V-grip and pull the bar (row it) to your ribs.

3. Leg Press

Sets: 1

Reps: As many as you can do in 60 seconds

Sit comfortably in the chair and position yourself so that your hips are beneath your knees and your knees are lined up with your feet. Choose a weight that you're sure you can lift at least 15 times. Remove the safety latches and lower your knees toward your chest until they are bent at a 90-degree angle. Then, press back up. You want to perform at least 15 reps but do as many as you can in 60 seconds. During Week 2, you'll increase the time for reps to 80 seconds. Then, in Week 3, you'll go for 100 seconds, and in Week 4, you'll do 120 seconds.

Stretch: Stretch out, particularly your lower body. Be sure to stretch hamstrings, quads, glutes, and hip flexors.

Day 2 Workout

1. A. Romanian Deadlift

Sets: 4
Reps: 8
Tempo: 4-0-X-0
Rest: 60 seconds

Step up to a barbell on the floor with your feet hip-width apart. Reach down and grab the bar with your hands shoulder-width apart. Lift the bar up along your shins and thighs until you are standing upright with your arms extended and the bar resting on your thighs. Now, bend at the hips keeping your back straight while you lower the bar about midway down your shins. You should feel a stretch in your hamstrings. Then, stand back up. Repeat.

1. B. Dumbbell Bench Press

Sets: 4
Reps: 8
Tempo: 4-0-X-0
Rest: 60 seconds

Lie on the weight bench with a dumbbell in each hand. Hold those weights at shoulder level with your arms at 45-degree angles from your sides. Press the weights straight up and lower them back again in a controlled manner.

2. A. Barbell Hip Thrust

Sets: 4

Reps: 8

Tempo: 4-0-X-0

Rest: 60 seconds

Sit on the floor and extend your legs. Rest your back on a bench. Roll a barbell up your thighs so that the bar sits on your lap. It might help to put a towel on your hips to cushion the weight. Bend your knees and brace your abs as you drive your heels into the floor. Extend your hips up until your butt and back are parallel to the floor. Lower back down in a controlled manner.

2. B. Pushups

Sets: 4

Reps: 8

Tempo: 4-0-X-0

Rest: 60 seconds

Get into the plank position with your hands on the floor shoulder-width apart and your feet close together. Brace your abs and draw your shoulder blades together as you lower your body until your chest is approximately one inch above the floor. Press back up.

3. Leg Curl

Sets: 1

Reps: As many as you can do in 60 seconds

Line your knees with the machine's axis of rotation. Choose a weight that you feel comfortable doing at least 15 reps. Curl the pad until your hamstrings are completely contracted. While you want to do at least 15 reps, you should strive to do as many as possible in 60 seconds. In Week 2, increase that time to 80 seconds. In Week 3, go for 100 seconds, and in Week 4, go for 120 seconds.

Stretch: Stretch out your lower body. Be sure to include hamstrings, quads, gluts, and hip flexors.

Day 3 Workout

1. A. Overhead Press

Sets: 4

Reps: 8

Tempo: 4-0-X-0

Rest: 60 seconds

Set the weight bar in a cage or squat rack. Grasp it with your hands a little more than shoulder-width apart. Lift the bar off the rack and bring it to shoulder level with your forearms perpendicular to the floor. Brace your abs as you squeeze the bar and press it overhead. Lower it back to shoulder level in a controlled manner.

1. B. Back Extension

Sets: 4

Reps: 8

Tempo: 4-0-X-0

Rest: 60 seconds

Lock your legs in the back-extension bench. Let your torso bend forward until your hips are at a 90-degree angle. Squeeze your glutes as you extend your hips until your body forms a straight line. Lower back down in a controlled manner.

2. A. Lateral Raise

Sets: 4

Reps: 8

Tempo: 4-0-X-0

Rest: 60 seconds

Stand while holding a dumbbell in each hand with your palms facing your sides. Raise the weights out at a 90-degree angle to your sides until your arms are parallel to the floor. Lower them back to the start position in a controlled manner.

2. B. Swiss-Ball Pike

Sets: 4

Reps: 8

Tempo: 4-0-X-0

Rest: 60 seconds

Begin in a pushup position but with your feet resting on a Swiss ball. Bend your hips so that your butt raises toward the ceiling. Continue until your torso is almost vertical and your hips are bent at a 90-degree angle. Lower back down in a controlled manner.

3. Resisted Sprint

Sets: 1

Reps: 8

Loop an exercise band around your waist and attack it to a sturdy object. Run in place with your legs pumping hard. Sprint hard for 10 seconds, then job lightly for 20 more seconds. That constitutes one rep. Continue until you complete all 8 reps. In Week 2, sprint for 12 seconds, jog for 18, in Week 3, sprint for 14 seconds, jog for 16 seconds, and in Week 4, spring for 16 seconds, jog for 14 seconds.

Stretch: As always, stretch out your lower body including your glutes, hamstrings, quads, and hip flexors.

Exercise Routine #2

This routine allows you to evenly train each of the major muscle groups without using weights. Instead, this routine combines HIIT cardio with compound strength-based exercises. It's a great way to increase your strength while at the same time improving your overall fitness, all without needing any equipment.

It works because by completing the exercises slower or faster or by doing extra reps or laps, you increase or decrease the intensity of the exercise so that you can do what's appropriate for you. Additionally, bodyweight exercises such as these involve a range of compound movements which serve to activate multiple muscles groups simultaneously. The following routine can be completed in 20 minutes or less, so even if you're short on time, this workout is for you.

Exercises #1 and #2: Inchworm and Pushup

These exercises are performed together back-to-back until you complete the superset three times. Then, you rest for one minute before moving on to the next three exercises. Each move is performed for 50 seconds and you rest for 10 seconds between each exercise. The last move is performed for 60 seconds.

Step 1: Inchworm--Stand with your feet shoulder-width apart. Bend at the hips and keep your legs as straight as possible until you are able to plant your hands on the floor directly in front of your feet. This is your start position. Walk your hands forward until you are in the plank position. Keep your legs straight and try not to raise your butt into the air.

Step 2: Pushup--Keep your back straight and stabilized by contracting your abdominal muscles as you bend your elbows and lower your torso toward the floor until your arms are at a 90-degree angle. Push using your chest muscles as you extend your arms to raise back into the plank position.

Step 3: Walk your hands back to the starting position without moving your feet. Keep your legs as straight as possible. This completes one rep. Do 15 reps, and then after a rest, begin a second and then third set.

Exercise #3: Crab Walk

Step 1: Stand with both feet hip-width apart while ensuring that your knees are in line with your toes. Look straight ahead and bend both the hips and the knees. Be sure to keep your knees in line with your toes. Bend until your upper legs are parallel to the floor. Keep your back at a 45-to-90-degree angle to your hips.

Step 2: While in the squat position, step your left foot out so that your feet are slightly more than shoulder-width apart. Stay in the squat position as you move your right foot inwards to bring your feet back to shoulder-width apart. That's one rep. Complete 15 reps on each side.

Exercises #4 and #5: Alternating Lunge and Twist

Step 1: Alternating lunge--place your forearms in front of your chest and stand with your feet shoulder-width apart.

Step 2: Take a large step forward with your left foot until both of your knees are bent at a 90-degree angle. Ensure that your weight is evenly distributed between both of your legs. Your front knee should be aligned with your ankle and your back knee should be hovering just off the floor.

Step 3: Twist--Now twist your torso so that your forearms are over your front leg. Make sure your knee remains in line with your middle toe. Twist back so that your forearms are once again in front of your chest.

Step 4: Transfer your weight to your right foot and step your left foot back to the starting position. That's one rep. Alternate between stepping your left foot forward and your right foot forward for 50 seconds.

Exercise #6: Deadbug

Step 1: Begin by lying on your back on a yoga mat. Extend your arms directly in front of your chest with your palms facing toward your feet. Bend your knees to bring your legs into the tabletop position. Make sure to keep your knees stacked over your hips and your shins parallel to the floor.

Step 2: Draw your ribs to your hips in order to engage the core. Bring your left arm down to the floor alongside your head while at the same time extending your right knee and hip to lower your right leg toward the floor but stop about an inch above the floor.

Step 3: Raise your left arm and right leg back to the start. That's one rep. Alternate sides for 50 seconds.

Exercise #7: Sprawls

Step 1: Place both feet more than shoulder-width apart and slightly pointed outward while standing on your yoga mat. Bend at the hips and knees until your upper legs are parallel to the floor. Make sure your knees are in line with your toes and that your back is at a 45-to-90-degree angle with your hips. Place your hands on the mat between your feet while keeping your spine in a neutral position. Jump both feet back so that your legs are completely extended and resting on the balls of your feet. Now, your body should be in a straight line from your head to your heels.

Step 2: Jump both feet forward between your hands. Release your hands as your raise back up to the starting position. That's one rep. Continue with reps for 50 seconds.

Exercise #8: Commando

Step 1: Start in a modified plank position with your forearms on the yoga mat and your legs extended behind you resting on the balls of your feet. Release your right forearm and place your hand flat on the mat beneath your shoulder. Push up onto your right hand and lift your left forearm to place your left hand on the mat directly beneath your shoulder.

Step 2: Release your right hand and lower your right forearm to the mat. Then release your left hand and lower your left forearm to the mat so that you are now back in the starting position. That's one rep. Continue to alternate between the left and right sides for 60 seconds.

These exercise routines are designed to help you get back into the routine after being away. They are certainly not the only routines you might choose, and as with any new exercise regimen, you should check with your doctor to make sure you're physically able to do these exercises. If, while exercising, you feel pain, nausea, dizziness, or any other alarming sensations, you should stop immediately and consult with your doctor.

Once you have gotten back into the groove with these exercises, you can begin to increase the length of your daily exercise routine and the intensity of the exercises. It's a good idea to pace yourself and don't try to do too much at once. You'll only burn out, and you'll be more likely to skip your workouts. Take it slow, and you'll be back on track for re-tuning your body. Now that we've got you back on the path to physical fitness, we'll take a look at recovering your social life in the next chapter.

REGAINING YOUR FRIENDS

A s I became more involved in my doomscrolling, I soon found my friends were avoiding me. That made me even gloomier and angrier. Once I realized, however, that it was my problem that initiated the distance between us, I knew I had to take steps to make things right. Once I had pulled my head out of the doomscrolling sand I had immersed myself in, I could see that I had let some good friendships get away from me. I became determined to make that right. Here's my tips to help you do the same.

Reconnecting

The first step is to reconnect with your friends. No matter how long it's been, you can still reach out and make yourself available for restarting the friendship. Don't wait for your friend to take that first step. Go ahead and just invite them to meet you somewhere. You can do that with a phone call or email. With one of my friends with whom I had been estranged for some time, I even wrote--yes, hand wrote--a letter. Just let them know that you've missed them, and you don't want to lose their friendship. You'll find they're probably as anxious as you to rekindle your relationship.

It is important to reach out in a proper way, and that kind of depends on the degree to which you've grown apart. It's also important just how good of a friend they were and the context of how you drifted apart. Was this a situation where you had just been ignoring them because of your obsession with doomscrolling or was there some kind of conflict or confrontation involved? If it's a situation where you just haven't really seen each other or talked in a while, you might casually reach out with an email or phone call. But if there was a conflict--as in my case--a letter might be a better way of approaching the situation.

I found that a letter allowed me to express my feelings about the conflict we had in a respectful way while at the same time expressing my desire to rekindle our friendship. I gave them the option of responding or not (they did) since I didn't want them to feel pressured. Whatever you do, the method you use should be more than just a text. Given that you haven't spoken in a while, it's really a situation that calls for something more substantial to emphasize your desire to reconnect.

Don't let the time apart be a reason for not reconnecting. In my case, it was 12 years! People fall out of touch for many different reasons, and just because it's been a long time, you shouldn't feel as though that means there's no hope. There are very few situations where a good friend wouldn't appreciate your desire to reconnect even if, ultimately, they decide they don't want to. Remember that you never know what's happened to your friend while you were apart. A lot can change in a short period of time. You might find you have more in common now than you ever did.

Also, the longer you wait, the more you're going to feel like you can't reach out. So, it's best just to swallow your pride and send that letter. Let them know that you value what you had together and that you hope they feel the same. Let bygones be bygones and start anew. Don't put undue pressure on them and be prepared to accept it if you don't hear back from them, but don't put it off any longer. You'll likely be glad you didn't wait.

Getting Back Together

It's understandable that you might be a little nervous when you actually go to get back together with your friend after it's been a while. You don't know what they'll be like or how they might have changed, and of course, you've also changed. So, the first thing to remember is that they will have changed. You can't expect them to be the same person. After all, you're not. It's always best to keep that first meeting short so that you can get the lay of the land. Meet for coffee or lunch instead of planning a night out. If all goes well, you can move on to that night out then.

You also want to meet someplace where you'll be comfortable, and you can hear each other without distractions. Since you were the one who got lost in the doomscrolling, it's best to apologize for your part in distancing yourself from your friendship. Let them know that you've come to realize just how that obsession took over your life and you're now working toward reinventing your life. Be honest with them about this and understand that they may have some negative emotions that still linger. Let them know that you are completely willing to listen to what they have to say and speak about what happened. You want to put the past behind you, but you have to let them express how they viewed the loss of your friendship.

As they speak about their own feelings, be respectful and listen with empathy to what they're saying. Practice active listening where you summarize what you hear them saying to ensure that is, in fact, what they mean. You also encourage them to continue talking with prompts like, "Yes," and, "I understand." Remember to use "I" statements when speaking about your own feelings. Try things like, "I feel like..." or, "I felt..." rather than, "You made me feel..." Additionally, don't be afraid to ask them to expand on a point if you don't fully understand what they're saying.

Another great way to spend that first meeting after a while apart is to recall some fond memories from your friendship. That will get you laughing together again and thinking about all the reasons you were friends in the first place. Take turns recalling some of the positive moments so that both of you can add your memories. This will certainly rekindle those positive feelings.

After Reconnecting

After you've reconnected and apologized for your part in the separation, it's time to forgive. This means forgiving any perceived transgressions on the part of your friend, but also forgiving yourself. Everyone's human, and friendships are complicated. Yes, you let your doomscrolling get in the way of your personal relationships. but that's not you anymore. You're different now, and it's time to move on. So, forgive yourself. If you feel your friends did something that you're not pleased about, forgive them even if they don't apologize.

Everyone is learning and growing through the different experiences of their lives, so by respecting each of your experiences, insights, and healing processes, you can move past any differences that might have contributed to your time apart. But you don't want to be making the same mistakes anew. Be sure that you follow through on the plans you make together going forward.

Your friend needs to know you're serious about reconnecting, and you show that by both making and keeping the plans you make together. If you commit to getting together, make sure you follow through. If something comes up, let them know immediately and make specific alternate plans. Try not to let that happen too often. Instead, when they ask you out, go! Make the time to spend time together, but don't be clingy.

Give your friend the space they need to grow again in the friendship. You need that too. So, keep your commitments, but also give each other space to grow back into the close relationship you once had. You might find you grow close again very quickly, but you might also find that you're really no longer compatible as friends. You both might have changed in different directions that just aren't agreeable for continuing a friendship. That's okay. Just be respectful and honest with them and leave the future open. You never know when you might reach out again and find something completely different.

Not every friendship will be the same nor will any friendship ever be perfect. Even your closest and best relationships will change over time, sometimes suddenly. That's not something you want to hold against a friend. You must accept them as they are now just as they must accept you. If you understand the nature of your friendship--is it casual, close, or simply an acquaintance--you can value each for its own gifts. You can also put more effort into those relationships where the feelings are reciprocated. That doesn't mean you disrespect the others, but you nurture what will grow in your life.

Give It Time

Remember that it takes time to build and rebuild a friendship. Let things play out naturally and at their own pace. You'll recover those friends who are important for your life now, and they'll help you grow as you reinvent your life following your doomscrolling addiction.

FINAL WORDS

Doomscrolling is an addictive behavior that can radically alter your life. I lost friends, my marriage suffered, my job suffered, and my outlook on life was terrible. Everything seemed like it was out to get me, and nothing seemed easy. It's a hard road back to a life you can enjoy, but it is worth the effort.

One of the most wonderful things I noticed when I had broken free of my doomscrolling habit was how vibrant everything seemed to be around me. I found I truly appreciated the little pleasures in life so much more than I had before. The sky was a brilliant blue and the flowers smelled so sweet! I hadn't realized just how dark my life had become. When I look back on it now, it seems like it happened to somebody else, and in a sense, it did. I am not that person anymore. I have hope in my life. I have direction, and I have optimism.

These are all things you will see too when you break that habit. There's a whole world of interesting, bright, and positive things that are just waiting for you to notice them. There are people who need you to truly be a part of their lives. They want and value your love and your friendship. They're missing you right now. It's time to come back to them.

You can break this habit and find the sun again. Your life doesn't have to be one negative news item after the next. The world may end, but probably not today. So, it's time to get back to your life. It's time to cut those virtual ties that bind and go outside to play with your children or walk with your spouse or talk with your friends.

Your doomscrolling is a habit, and like any habit, it can be broken. You can replace it with something that brings positive energy into your life, something that uplifts you even if the road is dark. Maybe all those bad things are going to happen, but all you can do is your part-- recycle, be kind to others, and love your family, for example--and keep living your life.

Be involved in your local community to really have an effect on those larger issues that concern you. The key is to stop reading about the problems and get involved in the solutions. Organize your community to make it greener or to ensure that there's equal opportunity. When that disaster strikes, organize your friends and family by getting them to donate needed materials or money to send to the victims. Volunteer for a relief organization. Stop reading and start doing. You may only see a small effect at first but give it time. It may grow into a global effort.

You only have control over your own actions. As you read about all the terrible things happening in the world, instead of going down that dark rabbit hole, get out into the sun and start doing something positive to help the situation. Maybe it won't amount to much, but it will be your effort. You will have done something about it. That will give you a sense of empowerment and even life purpose. It will also keep you connected to the real people in your life and your community. That's really all that matters here.

Those friends you have online, those people you follow on Twitter or Instagram, they're only pictures and words. You have real people in your life waiting for you to come be with them. They're waiting for you to remember what's really important. They're waiting for you to be their superhero. You can only do that when you get your head out of the sand and face the day. There's no better time than the present to get back to living your real life!

Printed in Great Britain
by Amazon